AF538305

ArtScroll Halachah Series®

Rabbi Nosson Scherman / Rabbi Meir Zlotowitz
General Editors

the
Lulav
Published by
Mesorah Publications, ltd

ספר פרי הדר

The Laws of the Four Species

Rabbi Hadar Margolin

Translated by

Rabbi Dovid Oratz

"THE LULAV AND ESROG HANDBOOK

First edition – First impression: September, 2003

Published by **MESORAH PUBLICATIONS, LTD.**
4401 Second Avenue / Brooklyn, NY 11232
(718) 921-9000 / Fax: (718) 680-1875 / www.artscroll.com

Distributed in Israel by SIFRIATI / A. GITLER
6 Hayarkon Street / Bnei Brak 51127 / Israel

Distributed in Europe by LEHMANNS
Unit E, Viking Industrial Park, Rolling Mill Road
Jarrow, Tyne and Wear, NE32 3DP / England

Distributed in Australia and New Zealand by GOLDS WORLD OF JUDAICA
3-13 William Street / Balaclava, Melbourne 3183, Victoria / Australia

Distributed in South Africa by KOLLEL BOOKSHOP
Shop 8A Norwood Hypermarket/ Norwood 2196 / Johannesburg, South Africa

Printed in the United States of America by
Edison Lithographing and Printing Corp.
Custom bound by Sefercraft, Inc. / 4401 Second Avenue / Brooklyn NY 11232

ISBN: 1-57819-380-X

Rabbi CHAIM P. SCHEINBERG
Rosh Hayeshiva "TORAH ORE"
and Morah Hora'ah of Kiryat Mattersdorf

הרב חיים פינחס שיינברג
ראש ישיבת "תורה אור"
ומורה הוראה דקרית מטרסדורף

בס"ד, י"ב במנחם אב, תשס"א

מכתב ברכה

הנה הביא לפני הרה"ג ר' הדר יהודה מרגולין שליט"א מפרי עמלו, קונטרס הנקרא בשם "פרי הדר", והוא מדריך מעשי על מצות ארבעת המינים, הדינים השייכים לכל מין ומין באופן מבואר ומאיר עינים, ומעוטר בציורים הממחישים את דיני ארבעת המינים לעיני המעיין, והכל עשה בצורה נאה, דבר דבור על אופניו, בטוב טעם ודעת.

והנה זה זמן רב שאיני יוצא בהסכמות לספרים, מטעם עמדי, ובפרט בספרים העוסקים בעניני הלכה, מ"מ בראותי את העמל שעל המחבר בקונטרס זה אמרתי לברכו שיזכה לחבר חיבורים נוספים בתורה הקדושה, להגדיל תורה בישראל ולהאדירה.

הכו"ח לכבוד התורה ולומדיה

חיים פינחס שיינברג

רחוב פנים מאירות 2, ירושלים, ת.ד. 6979, טל. 537-1513 (02), ישראל
2 Panim Meirot St., Jerusalem, P.O.B. 6979, Tel. (02) 537-1513, Israel

הרב ש. י. נסים קרליץ
רמת אהרן
רח' ר' מאיר 6, בני-ברק

בס"ד, יום ז' אלול תשס"א

כאשר הרב ר' הדר יהודה מרגולין שליט"א
עומד להוציא ספר על הל' ד' מינים בליווי
תמונות שיהיו לעזר ללימוד הלכות אלו כאשר
נצטוינו ללמוד הל' חג בחג ולקיים המצוות האלו
בהידור, הנני בזה לצרף ברכתי יזכה תמיד
לישב באהלה של תורה ולזכות את ישראל

ניסים קרליץ

כאשר ידידי הרב ר' הדר יהודה מרגולין שליט"א עומד להוציא ספר על הל' ד' מינים בליווי תמונות שיהיו לעזר ללימוד הלכות אלו כאשר נצטוינו ללמוד הלכות חג בחג ולקיים המצוות האלו בהידור. הנני בזה לצרף ברכתי יזכה תמיד לישב באהלה של תורה ולזכות את ישראל.

ניסים קרליץ

ב"ה

RABBI MOISHE STERNBUCH

Vice President "Eda Hacharedit"

And Dayan Jerusalem Beth-Din

Head Torah Centre Community

Johannesburg S.A.

משה שטרנבוך

סגן נשיא העדה החרדית בעיה"ק

מח"ס "מועדים וזמנים", "תשובות והנהגות" ועוד

ראב"ד דק"ק חרדים ביוהנסבורג

הכתובת בירושלים:

רח' משקלוב 13, הר-נוף, ירושלים

TeL: 6519610 :טל

בעזהי"ת, יום

קיבלתי ספרו של הרב המופלא ומופלג ה"ה הרב הדר מרגולין שליט"א (תושב שכונתנו הר נוף) וליקט דיני ד' מינים וסידר הדברים בליבון צח וקל לזכות הרבים, ויש כאן חכמה ומלאכה וראוי להפיצו שיביא תועלת בס"ד. והנני מצפה בכליון לישועת ה' ורחמי שמים מרובים.

משה שטרנבוך

הגאון רבי יהודה שפירא שליט״א

בס״ד אלול שנת השמיטה תשס״א

הרב היקר מוהר״ר הדר יהודה מרגולין שליט״א
מוציא לאור חיבור יקר על מצות ארבע מינים
בהדגמה ובציורים אשר יועילו ודאי לפרסם
הלכה ולימוד וידעת הדינים והספיקות
והריני לברכו שיצליח ויוציא לו עוד
חיבורים להגדיל תורה ולהאדירה
חותם למען כבוד התורה
והמחבר היקר
יהודא שפירא

הרב היקר מוהר״ר הדר יהודה מרגולין שליט״א מוציא לאור חיבור יקר על מצוות ארבע מינים בהדגמה ובציורים אשר יועילו ודאי לפרסם ההלכה ולימוד וידעת הדינים והספיקות והרני לברכו שיצליח ויוציא לו עוד חיבורים להגדיל תורה ולהאדירה.

חותם למען כבוד התורה
והמחבר היקר

יהודא שפירא

משה הלברשטאם
חבר הכד"צ העדה החרדית
ראש ישיבת "דברי חיים" משאקאווע
מח"ס שו"ת "דברי משה"
פעיה"ק ירושלים תובב"א
רח' יואל 8 טל. 5370514

בס"ד

ראיתי דברי הגאון האדיר מוהרח"פ שיינברג שליט"א אשר האריך בשבח המגיע לכתבי האברך הרה"ג מוה"ר הדר יהודה מרגולין שליט"א, אשר איתמחאי גברא ואיתמחאי קמיע בספריו הקודמים שהו"ל, ונתקבל תהלי"ת ברצון. ועתה דבר בעתו מה טוב חיבורו "פרי הדר" אשר יהא לתועלת לרבים וטובים ונטילת ישראל קדושים המחבבים את המצוות בבחי' זה א' ואנוהו התנאה לפניו העיקרים שיהא במצוות וכו' לולב נאה כאמז"ל (שבת קלג:) לדעת ליזהר בקניית כדת כדין וכהלכה. הד' מינים בחג הסוכות שיהא מהודר בשלימות ובעיקר במהרה ובכן ג"א מצטרפנא לברכו על פעלו הטוב, ויתן השי"ת ויפוצו מעיינותיו חוצה ויהי חלקו עם מצדיקי הרבים, ונתברך בסוכת שלום שיבנה דידן במכון בית א'.

משה הלברשטאם

יצחק מרדכי הכהן רובין
הר נוף עיה"ק ירושלים תובב"א

מוצש"ק לסדר "ראה אנוכי נותן
לפניכם היום ברכה", תשס"א

לכבוד
ידידי היקר מאוד נעלה
מחשובי באי בית מדרשנו
הרה"ג ר' הדר יהודה מרגולין שליט"א
בעמח"ס הדרן עלך וכו'

אחדשה"ט
שמחתי לראות ששוב הנך בא לזכות את כלל ישראל המהדרין במצוות, והפעם בספר בענין ארבעת המינים אשר "פרי הדר" יקרא, וכו השכלת להביא בקצירת אמרים את עיקרי ההלכות המצויות בדינים אלו בלשון השוה לכל נפש למען ירוץ הקורא בו, וכן תמונות המאירות עינים להבין את המציאות של כל הלכה והלכה, גם לרבות הוראות מגדולי ישראל אשר מפיהם אנו חיים.
ישבתי זמן זמנים טובא עם הרב הנ"ל ועברנו על הכת"י מרישא לסיפא ונוכחתי לדעת שספר זה יהיה רב התועלת ובפרט לאלה אשר זמנם אין איתם לעבור על הלכות אלו בעיון ורוצים לדעת בקצרה את עיקרי הדברים למען יוכלו לחבב המצוה ולחפש בעצמם ד' מינים כשרים ומהודרים ולא יצטרכו לקנותם סגורים וחתומים.
וברכתי ברכת כהן שתזכה להמשיך וללון בד' אמות של הלכה ולזכות את עם ישראל בעוד חיבורים טובים ומועילים.

ביקרא דאורייתא
יצחק מרדכי הכהן רובין

רח' שאולזון 62 הר-נוף ירושלים 95400 טל. 518525

contents

Introduction

I humbly offer a song of praise to Hashem, Who has given me the privilege to publish my book, *The Lulav and Esrog Handbook,* on the mitzvah of the Four Species.

There are many detailed laws concerning the Four Species, and a person must study long and hard to achieve a clear and practical understanding of these laws. Nevertheless, there are many other obligations during the month of Tishrei which greatly reduce the amount of time available for the average person to sit peacefully and to carefully study each law as befits a subject of this nature. Furthermore, it is sometimes hard to accurately understand a physical feature based on its verbal description in the halachic works, so it may be difficult to translate the law into practical guidelines for finding a kosher set of Four Species.

In this work, we have tried to focus on the most common laws from a practical perspective, so that a person can know what is most important when purchasing the Four Species. We have also cited the opinions of the halachic authorities concerning common issues that are not explicitly discussed in *Mishnah Berurah*.

It must be emphasized that a work of this limited scope is meant to provide guidelines, and not to rule in halachic matters. Only a qualified rabbi with experience in these matters can decide specific questions.

May it be His will that this book prove useful, and that we succeed in presenting the *halachos* clearly and accurately.

❖ ❖ ❖

The importance of teaching *halachah* through illustration is found in the Torah. Regarding the classification of kosher and nonkosher animals, the Torah says (*Vayikra* 11:2), "This is the animal that you may eat." *Rashi* explains that the term "this" indicates that Moshe would hold up each animal, show it to Israel and say, "This you may eat and this you may not eat." *Maharal,* in *Gur Aryeh* (ad loc.), explains that, "Since there are both pure and impure animals, it is necessary to present them visually so that all can become expert in them."

Here too, the reader can understand more clearly when the laws are presented through photographs and illustrations.

❖ ❖ ❖

As mentioned above, this book is not meant to be a comprehensive treatment of all the laws of the Four Species. Rather, it is meant to be a handbook for the most common practical applications. Accordingly, the sources are discussed only briefly. Anyone interested in a more comprehensive discussion can easily find the source in *Shulchan Aruch* and its major commentaries, and in the other excellent works written on this subject.

Three exceptionally useful books should be mentioned; indeed, I made much use of them in this work:

(A) *Arbaas HaMinim,* by Rabbi Eliahu Weissfish *shlita,* an encyclopedic storehouse on the mitzvah of the Four Species.

(B) *Kashrus Arbaas HaMinim,* by Rabbi Yechiel Michel Stern *shlita* (available in English translation as *Halachos of the Four Species*), a detailed discussion of the laws of the Four Species, accompanied by photographs.

(C) *Hilchos Chag BeChag* on the Four Species, by Rabbi Moshe Mordechai Karp *shlita,* a detailed discussion of the laws through analysis of the *poskim.*

Acknowledgments

It is difficult to sufficiently thank my rebbi, HaGaon HaRav Yitzchak Mordechai HaKohen Rubin *shlita,* Rav and *poseik* in my community of Har Nof, Jerusalem, and author of *Marei Kohen* on the laws of *niddah.* Not only did he encourage me in this work, but he also reviewed the entire Hebrew work to ensure that the laws were presented precisely and clearly. Indeed, most of this book is based upon the Rav's public lectures. (It should be noted that the rulings of R' Shlomo Zalman Auerbach *zatzal,* and [may they live long lives] R' Yosef Shalom Eliashiv *shlita* and R' Shmuel Wosner *shlita* were heard from them by Rabbi Rubin.) May I humbly bless Rabbi Rubin *shlita* that Hashem repay his efforts and that his wellsprings continue to overflow, thereby spreading Torah and glorifying it.

I am also indebted to Rabbi Shmuel Sheinelson *shlita* (author of *Shaarei Halachah* on the laws of *ribbis*) and to Rabbi Shevach Zvi Rosenblatt *shlita,* who reviewed this work from beginning to end. Many of their comments are reflected in the text.

I am most thankful to Rabbi Yitzchak Kaufman *shlita* for all his assistance.

I express my heartfelt gratitude to Rabbi Dovid Oratz *shlita,* who expertly rendered this book into English, and to

Rabbi Menachem Goldman *shlita,* who reviewed and made valuable comments on the English manuscript.

❖ ❖ ❖

I would also like to thank Avraham and Gitel Esther Zolty, and Dr. Eli and Cheryl Prenzlau, who assisted me in publishing the Hebrew edition of this book. A separate heartfelt thanks to Avraham Menachem Schijveschuurder, whose help was dedicated to honor the memory of his brother, sister-in-law and three of their children who died sanctifying the Name of Hashem in the horrific bombing of the Sbarro Pizzeria in Central Jerusalem in the summer of 2001.

יוֹם טוֹב שֵׁנִי / Yom Tov Sheni

Jews who live outside Israel observe a second day of Succos similar to the first. This day is known as *Yom Tov Sheni* (the second festival day).

In general, all disqualifications that apply on the first day apply to *Yom Tov Sheni* as well. However, if replacements are not reasonably available, one may use species with first-day disqualifications without reciting the *berachah* over them (*Shulchan Aruch* 649:5 and *Mishnah Berurah* #50).

A note regarding references

Throughout each chapter, references to *Shulchan Aruch* that do not cite a specific *siman* refer to the *siman* dealing with the species under discussion. For esrog this is *Siman* 648, for lulav 645, for hadassim 646, and for aravos 647.

a summary of the laws of the four species

A Summary of the Laws of the Four Species

Introduction

This digest serves two purposes:

As an index, organized in the order of the main body of the book, so that a specific law can be easily located by looking at the page reference at the end of the paragraph; and

As a summary, to allow quick review of the main parts of the laws.

One should not rely on this section alone, as not all the details of each law are given here.

☙ Esrog

(A) Certification

Purchase an esrog with a הֶכְשֵׁר [*hechsher*], certification, that it is neither grafted nor prohibited to be eaten. Note whether the certification also warrants that this specific esrog was inspected and found to be kosher. (See p. 31.)

(B) Color change

שִׁנּוּי מַרְאֶה [*Shinui mareh*], a color change (to a disqualifying color; see below) disqualifies an esrog in one of three circumstances:

(1) Majority: When it covers a majority of the esrog. (See p. 33.)

(2) Two or three spots: When the color is changed on two or three spots that comprise the majority of the esrog's circumference, so that the change in color is visible from any angle at which the esrog is viewed.[1] (See p. 33.)

(3) On the חֹטֶם, *chotem*: When there is a visible change in color, of any size, on the *chotem*. The emphasis is on "visible"; if the spot is so tiny that it cannot be seen with the unaided eye without great scrutiny, it does not disqualify the esrog. The *chotem* is the part of the esrog that slopes upward to the פִּיטָם, *pitam*, and includes the *pitam*. (See p. 34.)

(C) Colors that disqualify

The colors that disqualify an esrog are: (a) certain types of black; (b) white (but not beige); and (c) dark green (on a yellow esrog). There is disagreement among the *poskim* (halachic authorities) as to whether two or three spots of a different color (brown-red, light green, etc.) on the esrog disqualify it; the majority view is to be lenient. (See p. 35.)

When part of an esrog peels off and the area underneath turns brown, many treat it as a disqualifying color. Nevertheless, a color change to brown because of a bruise does not disqualify the esrog. (See p. 37.)

Leaf marks (marks that are usually a light cream color) do not disqualify the esrog, but they do reduce its quality. (See p. 39.)

---

1. This can also apply to two spots that are positioned on opposite sides of the esrog, if they are large enough so they can be seen from any angle.

A wartlike protuberance the same color as the esrog is not a חֲזָזִית, *chazazis,* and does not disqualify the esrog. (See p. 41.) [*Chazazis* is a scablike growth indicating rot and spoilage. It disqualifies the esrog, but is rarely found today.]

(D) An incomplete esrog

The tiniest quantity missing from an esrog disqualifies the esrog as חָסֵר [*chaseir*], incomplete, but only on the first day of Succos. On *Yom Tov Sheni,*[2] such an esrog may be used even with a *berachah*, as long as the hole (a) does not go completely through the esrog or (b) is not the size of an *issar* coin. When only some of the thin external peel is missing, the esrog is kosher, but if any of the second peel is missing, the esrog is disqualified, as stated above. If, however, a membrane grows over the missing part, it is kosher even for the first day. (See p. 42.)

A broken פִּיטָם, *pitam*: If all of the *pitam* breaks off and leaves an indentation in the top of the esrog, some say that it is disqualified for all seven days. If only part of it breaks off and the portion that remains protrudes above the top of the esrog, the esrog is kosher, but it is preferable to use a different esrog on all seven days. If this was the type of *pitam* that grows from the esrog itself, the esrog is disqualified for the first day when any part of the *pitam* falls off. As with any incomplete esrog, if a replacement is unavailable, one may use it on *Yom Tov Sheni* without reciting the *berachah.*

A *pitam* that fell off the esrog as part of the normal growth process while the esrog was on the tree does not affect the status of the esrog in any way and it is perfectly acceptable for use. (See p. 45.)

A missing stem: If the עֹקֶץ [*oketz*], stem, of the esrog breaks off, as long the stem hole is fully covered, the esrog

2. For explanation of *Yom Tov Sheni,* see p. 18.

is kosher. (See p. 47.)

(E) The size of an esrog

The required minimum size of an esrog is כְּבֵיצָה [*kebeitzah*], the size of an egg (most of the esrogim available today are at least this size). (See p. 49.)

(F) A green esrog

Though some authorities are stringent regarding using an esrog that is dark green, the prevalent custom is to allow such an esrog to be used. (See p. 49.)

See a practical guide for examining an esrog on p. 51.

◆§ Lulav

According to *Shulchan Aruch*, the disqualifications of a lulav only apply when they affect the שִׁדְרָה, *shidrah,* or most of the leaves. Lulavim today rarely have such disqualifications.

According to *Rema*, however, the disqualifications apply even if only the תְּיוֹמֶת [*teyomes*], the central leaf, is affected. All the disqualifications we discuss regarding the lulav are according to the custom of Ashkenazi Jews, which follows the opinion of *Rema*. (See p. 55.)

(A) A split *teyomes*

When most of the length of the *teyomes* (the central double-leaf) is split (i.e., the two sides of the double-leaf came apart), the lulav is disqualified; if less than half the length of the *teyomes* is split, the lulav is kosher. On Chol HaMoed (the Intermediate Days of the Festival), the lulav is kosher even if a majority is split, but it is appropriate to be stringent. (See p. 56.)

Ideally: One should avoid using a lulav with a *teyomes* that is even slightly split, out of concern that, as the lulav is used, the split may spread to most of the *teyomes*. Contemporary halachic authorities consider a partially-split *teyomes* that has been glued together — to prevent the split from spreading

— to still be מְהֻדָּר [*mehudar*], ideal. (See p. 59.)

(B) A הִמְנָק, *himnak,* split

When the tips of a partially-split *teyomes* face opposing directions so that the lulav seems to end in two separate tops, the lulav is disqualified for use on the first day. If a replacement is unavailable, one may use it on *Yom Tov Sheni* without reciting the *berachah.* It is preferable to avoid using such a lulav on the other days as well.

There is even reason not to use a lulav if only the leaves adjacent to the central *teyomes* are split this way. (See p. 59.)

(C) קוֹרָא, *Kora; moich*

A lulav with a brownish-red covering (*kora* or *moich*) over its upper leaves is kosher. Some actually prefer using such a lulav, while others avoid it. Ashkenazi Jews should remove this covering from the leaves alongside the top טֶפַח, *tefach,* of the *shidrah,* so that the leaves can shake when the lulav is waved. (See p. 62.)

(D) Withered

A withered lulav (יָבֵשׁ, *yaveish*) may not be used, but only if it is dry to the point at which the leaves are white, with no trace of greenness. (See p. 63.)

Some say that according to *Raavad* even if only the central leaf is this dry the lulav is disqualified. Others disagree.

A lulav that has a tip that was burned by the sun is not disqualified, provided that the area maintains its firmness. (See p. 63.)

(E) Zigzag tip

A lulav with a zigzag tip is generally permitted. However, one must be more careful when checking the tip, since it is common for the *teyomes* to be split. (See p. 65.)

(F) Single-leafed *teyomes*

A lulav with a *teyomes* that is not a doubled leaf is disqualified. When one of the two sides of the double-leaf is narrower than the other, the lulav is kosher if the narrower leaf covers most of the broader one. Similarly, when one side does not reach the top of the other, the lulav is kosher provided that the majority is covered. Some are more stringent in this matter. (See p. 66.)

(G) Length

The *shidrah* should be four טְפָחִים [*tefachim*], handbreadths, long (between 12.6 and 15.75 inches). When binding the hadassim and aravos with the lulav, take care that the top handbreadth of the *shidrah* is above the tops of the other two species. (See p. 67.)

(H) The tip of the *teyomes*

When the tip of the *teyomes* is fully bent, so that the end faces downward, the custom is to permit the lulav, in accordance with the ruling of *Shulchan Aruch.* Though *Rosh* preferred such a lulav, others disqualify it. If the tip only bends forward, but does not face down, all agree that it is fully acceptable (מְהֻדָּר, *mehudar*). (See p. 69.)

(I) A curved lulav

A bent lulav is kosher unless it is so curved that it is sicklelike. Even a sicklelike lulav is kosher, however, if the curve is to the back, in the direction of the *shidrah*. (See p. 70.)

(J) Cut-off top

A lulav with a cut-off top *(נִקְטַם ראשו, niktam rosho)* is disqualified. Nevertheless, as long as the cut is not apparent under close scrutiny, the lulav is not disqualified. If only the needlelike projection on top of the lulav is cut off, the lulav is kosher. (See p. 71.)

Hadas

(A) Triple-leaved

A hadas must be triple-leaved to be kosher. If the three leaves do not emerge from the same level of the stem, it is not considered triple-leaved. (See p. 75.)

"Emerging from the same level" is defined by some as three leaves that recognizably belong to the same level. Others are careful that the stems should emerge from the branch at the same level. Even according to this view, however, as long as one straight line connects the stems, it is kosher. (See p. 75.)

If part of a leaf tears off but the majority remains, the leaf is considered complete. (See p. 80.)

(B) Length of a hadas

Preferably, the length of the branch of a hadas should be three טְפָחִים [*tefachim*], handbreadths (between 9.45 and 11.8 inches).

When necessary, one can use a hadas that is at least 2.5 *tefachim*. (See p. 77.)

(C) A majority (lengthwise)

Ideally, all three *tefachim* of the hadas should be triple-leaved. Nevertheless, the hadas is fully kosher as long as a majority of its required length is triple-leaved — even if the top of the hadas is not. "Most of three *tefachim*" comes out to about 5 inches according to R' Chaim Naeh, 5.5 inches according to R' Moshe Feinstein, and 6 inches according to the *Chazon Ish*. (See p. 77.)

When an area in the middle of the hadas is not triple-leaved, the hadas is kosher as long as the triple-leaved areas above and below add up to the required length. (See p. 78.)

[One should be careful, when placing the hadassim and aravos into the holder, not to rip off any leaves.]

(D) A majority (widthwise)

When one of the three leaves falls off at a given level, some still consider that area to be "triple-leaved"; others disagree. (See p. 79.)

(E) Withered

A hadas whose leaves turn white is considered dry (יָבֵשׁ, *yaveish*) and is disqualified. As long as the leaves maintain some green color, however, they are not considered to be dry. Hadassim almost always maintain their green color throughout the season in which they were cut. (See p. 81.)

(F) Cut-off top

If the top of the hadas branch is cut off (נִקְטַם, *niktam*), it is better not to use the hadas. If only the top leaves were cut off, this does not apply. (See p. 81.)

☙ Aravah

(A) The length of aravos

Aravos have the same required length as hadassim; see above. (See p. 85.)

(B) Missing leaves

If most of the leaves are missing, the aravah is disqualified; otherwise, it is kosher. Nevertheless, some prefer that the aravah not be used unless all the leaves are intact. (See p. 86)

(C) Withered

An aravah leaf is only considered dry (*yaveish*) if there is no greenness left as a result of dryness. Even so, the aravah is disqualified only when a majority of it is this dry. In any case it is preferable to use only fresh aravos. (See p. 86.)

(D) Cut-off top

If the top of the aravah branch was cut off (*niktam),* the aravah is disqualified. (See p. 87.)

Lavluv: A young leaf growing from the top of the branch indicates that the top was not cut off, but does not affect the status of the aravah. (See p. 87.)

ESROG

ולקחתם לכם
ביום הראשון
פרי עץ הדר
כפות תמרים
ענף עץ עבות
וערבי נחל

ESROG

◆§ The Need for Certification

An esrog that is מֻרְכָּב [*murkav*], the product of grafting, is not considered an esrog at all. It is disqualified for use on all the seven days of Succos (*Mishnah Berurah* 648:65).

An esrog which is prohibited to be eaten — such as an esrog of עָרְלָה *orlah*(grown during the first three years of the tree, when the use of its fruits is prohibited) or an esrog of *tevel* טֶבֶל (untithed produce) — is also disqualified for all seven days (*Shulchan Aruch* 649:5, *Mishnah Berurah* 45).

Accordingly, one must be certain to purchase an esrog that is free of these disqualifications. Nowadays, many esrogim (the plural of esrog) carry certification warranting that they are ungrafted and permitted for eating. The certification may be that of a reliable rabbinic organization, a qualified rabbi, or even that of a trustworthy seller who has mastered all the relevant laws. (It is not sufficient for the seller to be an expert on esrog trees, he must be equally expert in the laws of tithing as well as the laws of *orlah.*[1]) One should only purchase an esrog with such certification.

1. For example, a new branch that comes out from beneath the ground is considered like a "new tree" and an esrog that grows from that branch is considered *orlah* until three years pass from when that branch first emerged.

In addition, many esrogim carry a certification that they have been examined and meet *all* the requirements of a kosher esrog. Though this certification is by no means necessary, it does make purchasing an esrog simpler. This certification will usually grade the esrog, labeling it as "kosher enough to recite the blessing over"; "כָּשֵׁר לְכַתְּחִלָּה [*kosher lechatchilah*], absolutely kosher"; or "מְהֻדָּר [*mehudar*], beautiful," (as well as various degrees of *mehudar*).

Although an esrog with this additional level of certification requires no further examination, certain problems which affect the esrog's acceptability and its level of הִדּוּר [*hiddur*], beauty, can arise during transport. Therefore, any questions regarding even a certified esrog must be referred to a rabbi with expertise in this area.

Pedigree

Any esrog which has a known presumption (*chazakah*) to be ungrafted is kosher. Nevertheless, there are certain varieties of esrog considered to be of "known pedigree," and that are "certainly" not grafted.

שִׁנּוּי מַרְאֶה / Change in Appearance

The basis for the laws concerning *shinui mar'eh,* changes in an esrog's appearance, is the Gemara's discussion of חֲזָזִית [*chazazis*] (*Succah* 35b, see *Mishnah* 34b).

A *chazazis* is a scablike protuberance on the skin of the esrog (*Shulchan Aruch* 648:13) that comes as a result of rot and spoilage (*Beur Halachah* ad loc.). It is rarely found in esrogim today, but its laws apply to other forms of color change that are considered similar to *chazazis.*

The size of a spot that disqualifies

A *chazazis,* or a color change considered similar to *chazazis,* disqualifies the esrog in one of three circumstances: (a) when it covers a majority of the esrog, (b) when it is in two or three different spots, or (c) when it is on the חֹטֶם [*chotem*] (see below). Since *chazazis* is rarely found on esrogim today, we will limit the rest of our discussion to changes in color and appearance.

The "changes in color" discussed in the following rules refer only to the colors described below, which are similar to *chazazis*.

(a) Majority

A change in color over a majority of the esrog's area disqualifies the esrog (*Shulchan Aruch* 648). This is quite uncommon.

(b) Two or three spots

Three spots that cover the majority of the esrog's circumference on the lower part of an esrog (see "On the *chotem*," below, regarding the top of the esrog) disqualify the esrog (ibid. and *Mishnah Berurah* §41). This is because a person can see about half of the esrog at a time, and when the spots cover a majority of the circumference,[2] the changes in appearance are visible from any angle from which the esrog is viewed.[3]

If, however, the esrog can be held so that the spots are not apparent to a person viewing the esrog (i.e., the three spots are on the opposite side), the esrog is not disqualified.

Two spots can also disqualify the esrog if they are opposite one another and each one is somewhat large. In that case too, the end result is a change in color that is visible from any angle from which the esrog is viewed.

---

2. One should be careful in measuring the circumference. If there is a bump on the far side of the esrog, the circumference is increased and the part on the far side is correspondingly greater.

3. According to *Chazon Ish* (147:5), one may be lenient as long as the color changes are not spread over a majority of the esrog's area (i.e., if a circle were to be drawn to encompass all the discolored areas, the circle would not cover most of the esrog).

(c) On the *chotem*

A spot of any size on the חֹטֶם [*chotem*], (lit. "nose"), disqualifies the esrog. The *chotem* is the part of the esrog that slopes upward to the פִּיטָם [*pitam*] [see below for definition of *pitam*] (*Shulchan Aruch* 648:10-12). The *pitam* itself is considered part of the *chotem* (*Beur Halachah* ad loc. s.v. *mimakom*).[4] Because the *chotem* is the part that people generally see when they look at an esrog, the rules for disqualification are more stringent there than for the rest of the esrog (see *Rashi on Succah* 35b s.v. *uvechotmo*).

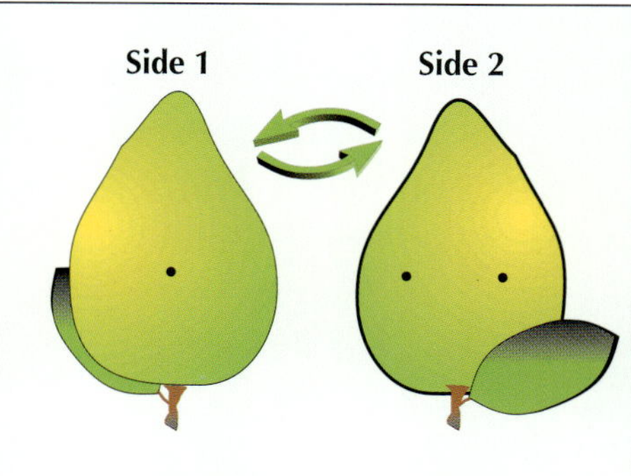

An esrog with three dots

If at least one of the dots can be seen from any angle, the esrog is disqualified.

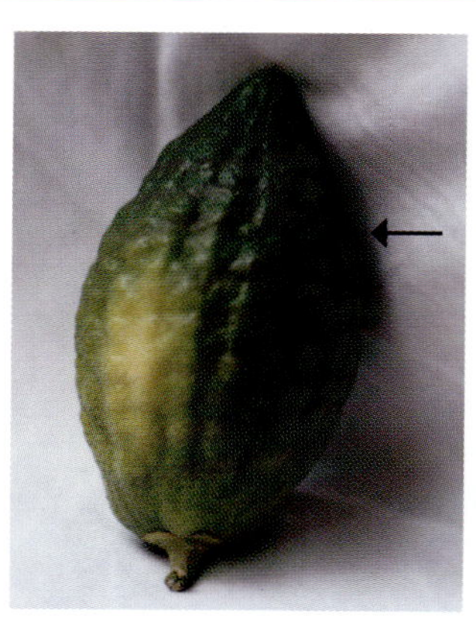

The חֹטֶם / *chotem*

The *chotem* is the part of the esrog that slopes upward to the top. The arrows in the pictures indicate the beginning of the slope. A color change to a disqualifying color, regardless of its size, disqualifies the esrog when it is on the *chotem*.

4. Concerning the definition of the *chotem* after the first day, see *Bikkurei Yaakov* 649:30.

What is considered visible?

Not visible without scrutiny

A spot which is too small to be visible from the distance that an esrog is normally held does not disqualify the esrog.

Since these disqualifications are based on what people see, the spot must be clearly visible. Thus, if the spot is so tiny that it cannot be seen by the unaided eye without great scrutiny, it does not disqualify the esrog (*Mishnah Berurah* §46).

The accepted definition of "not visible without scrutiny" is a spot that is not visible when held as far away from the eye as an esrog is normally held (*Mabit* III:49; *Graz* 648:22; *Pri Megadim, Eishel Avraham,* s.v. *ketzas dinei esrog; Shaar HaTziyun* 648:49).

Needless to say, a spot that can only be detected under a magnifying glass does not affect the acceptability or the הִדּוּר *[hiddur],* (beauty), of an esrog.

The colors that disqualify

(a) Black

Black spots that can be easily lifted without removing any of the outer peel do not disqualify the esrog.

Some black spots that cannot easily be removed have the same status as a *chazazis* (*Shulchan Aruch* 648:12, 16), and all the rules discussed regarding size and location of *chazazis* apply to them. There is a disagreement among *poskim* whether other black spots, common on esrogrim, have this status as well. A competent Rav must therefore be consulted regarding any black spots that cannot be lifted without damaging the outer peel.

(b) White

A white spot is considered similar to a *chazazis* (ibid.:16). This applies only to pure white, which is defined by *Maharsham* (*Daas Torah* 648) as the color of hard-boiled egg white (or the white of an eggshell). An off-white color does not disqualify the esrog (the accepted ruling of *Chazon Ish* and the current ruling of R' Y. S. Eliashiv *shlita*). [However, see *Daas Torah* op. cit. who rules stringently regarding off-white on the first day of Succos.] Beige spots, which are common on the esrog, certainly do not disqualify the esrog.

(c) Dark green

Spots that are as green as grass also disqualify an esrog as a *chazazis* would (*Mishnah Berurah* §55), even when the rest of the esrog is yellow. A fully green esrog will be discussed below, p. 49.

(d) Other colors

Spots of other colors (such as brown, light green, yellow, or red) are not considered similar to a *chazazis.* However, when the color is not a standard color for an esrog and it appears in two or three places over the circumference of the esrog (as explained above, "The size of a spot that disqualifies," page 32), some authorities disqualify the esrog as מְנֻמָּר [*menumar*], "spotted" (see *Mishnah Berurah* §55). However, *Shaar HaTziyun* (ad loc. §62) cites the *Gra* as

Brown

A brown discoloration does not disqualify the esrog.

ruling leniently with regard to these colors, and understands the *Shulchan Aruch* as ruling leniently as well.[5]

Yellow spots on a green esrog

The yellow spots on a green esrog are generally a result of a leaf having covered that area during the growth of the esrog, preventing that area from receiving sunshine. Such spots do not disqualify the esrog even when they cover many areas on the esrog.

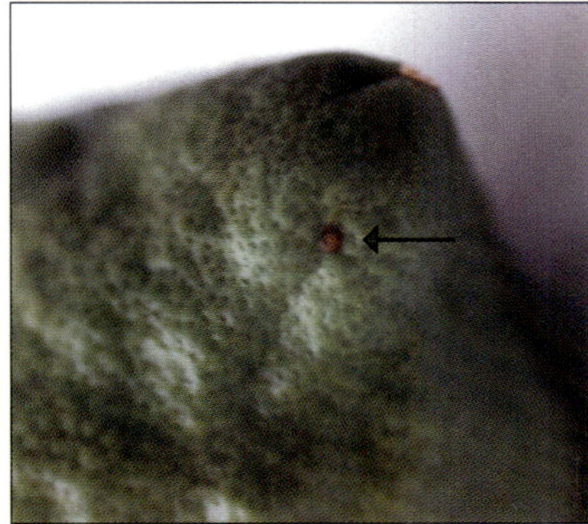

A citrus insect

The brown "spot" in this picture is actually not part of the esrog. It appears as a bulge on the surface of the esrog and is a citrus insect, which does not disqualify the esrog. The insect can be removed by carefully scraping it with a matchstick, and the remaining white sticky substance may be washed off the esrog.

A color change resulting from peeling of the external thin peel

When part of the external thin peel of an esrog peels off, the area generally turns brown or beige as a reaction to the acidic juice (see below).

While this does not disqualify the esrog as חָסֵר [*chaseir*], incomplete (see below p. 42), according to some authorities it will disqualify the esrog because of the resulting change in

5. According to R' M. Heller *zt"l* of Yerushalayim, many of today's halachic authorities rule leniently on this point.

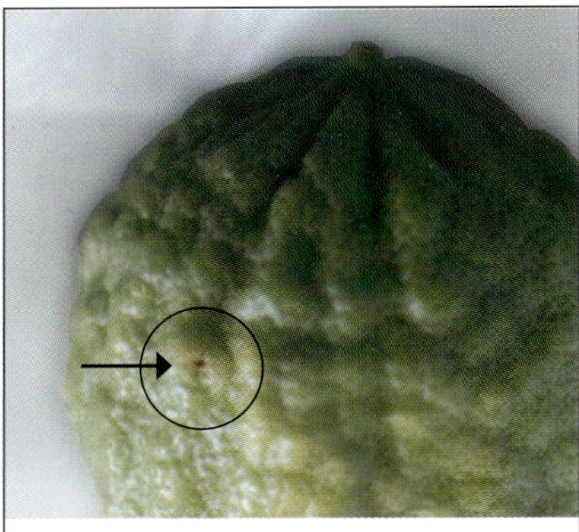

Brown spots

Brown spots are often caused when the acidic juice of the esrog is released and interacts with the surface of the esrog. Such spots do not disqualify the esrog, but they do detract from its overall quality.

color (despite the fact that the change is to an acceptable color) if the peeled spot is on the *chotem* or if it is in two or three spots (as explained above). *Mishnah Berurah* §26 rules that when another esrog is not reasonably available, one may rely on the lenient opinion.

According to the stringent opinion, this disqualification applies to all seven days of Succos. (See note 7 below for further discussion of this point.)

This type of color change commonly results when people try to remove a black spot on the esrog and, in the process, remove a part of the external peel or otherwise bruise the surface. The acidic juice that is released interacts with the surface of the esrog and causes a brown spot.

A color change resulting from a bruise

Any bruise can cause the release of the acidic juice which then interacts with the surface and causes a brown spot (see top picture on following page). Such a spot does not disqualify the esrog (*Chazon Ish* 147). It does, however, mitigate the הָדָר [*hadar*], beauty, quality of the esrog.

It takes several hours (up to two days) for the brown spot to appear. Accordingly, whenever the esrog is bruised in any way (and certainly when a piece of the outer peel peels off), it is recommended that one rinse the esrog in water to prevent the acidic juice from interacting with the surface of the esrog. This will usually prevent a brown spot from developing.

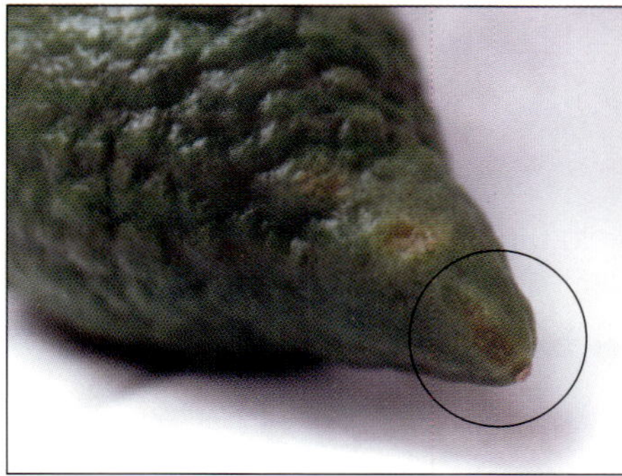

Brown Stains

The brown stain in the picture was caused by the acidic juice released when the esrog was bruised. The stain does not disqualify the esrog, but it does detract from its overall quality.

Leaf marks *(bletlach)*

When a leaf or branch scrapes gently on the surface of an esrog during its growth, the healing process causes beige scars to grow on the surface of the esrog. These scars are colloquially referred to as *bletlach* (singular: *bletl*). *Bletlach* do not disqualify an esrog because generally they are not raised from the surface of the esrog (see below), and are therefore not considered similar to *chazazis* (see page 32). Furthermore, because of their prevalence they are considered part of an esrog's normal appearance (*Rema* 648:13). Although the *bletlach* do not disqualify an esrog, they do mitigate the *hadar* (beauty) quality of the esrog (*Pri Megadim,* end of 648).

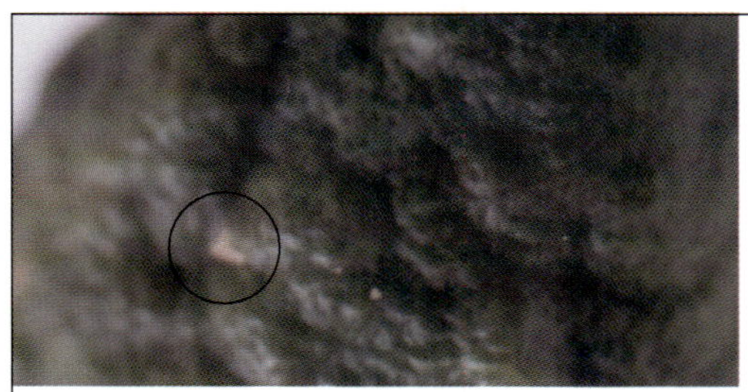

Leaf marks *(bletlach)*

Bletlach are commonly found cream, beige, or off-white scars on the surface of an esrog. They do not disqualify the esrog, but they do detract from its overall quality.

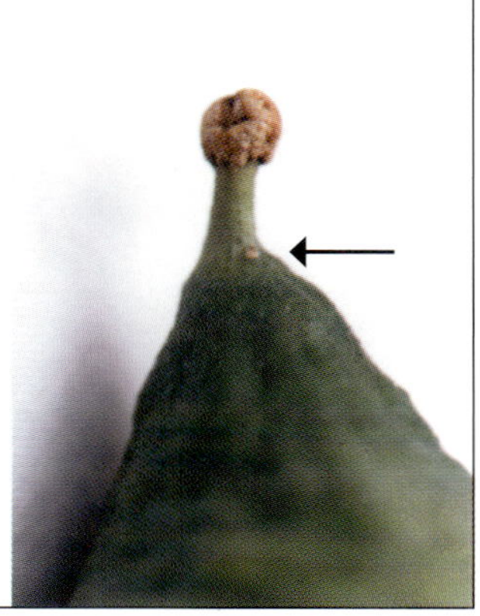

Leaf marks *(bletlach)*

Bletlach are commonly found cream, beige, or off-white scars on the surface of an esrog. They do not disqualify the esrog, but they do detract from its overall quality.

If a *bletl* is raised from the surface of the esrog, the esrog may be used only if it is difficult to acquire a replacement (*Mishnah Berurah* §50). This applies only to a *bletl* that is quite noticeably raised; a slight irregularity felt by running one's fingers along the surface does not count. In fact, one is unlikely to come across an esrog with *bletlach* that are quite noticeably raised.

A wartlike protuberance

Sometimes an esrog can have a wartlike protuberance (see picture below). When its color is the same as the color of the esrog it is not considered a *chazazis,* and the esrog is kosher (though not ideal). The reason for this is that a *chazazis* results from rot and spoilage, and as long as the color of the protuberance is the same as the rest of the esrog one can be certain that spoilage is not involved.[6]

A wartlike protuberance

Since the color is the same as the rest of the esrog, it is not considered a *chazazis* and it does not disqualify the esrog. It does, however, detract from its overall quality.

Side view of the same protuberance.

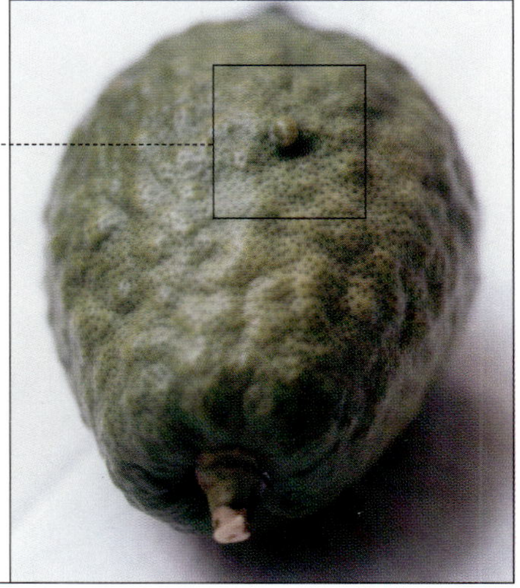

6. One should nevertheless be careful when handling such an esrog to ensure that he not scrape the area, thereby causing a color change or a deficiency.

◈ חָסֵר / An Incomplete Esrog

Even the tiniest quantity missing from an esrog disqualifies the esrog as *chaseir,* incomplete (*Shulchan Aruch* 648:2, first opinion). This disqualification applies only to the first day of Succos.[7] On *Yom Tov Sheni*[8] one may use such an esrog, even with a *berachah,* as long as (a) it is not a hole that goes completely through the esrog or (b) the missing portion is smaller than an *issar*[9] coin. When no other esrog is available, one may use such an esrog even on the first day. On the other days of Succos, however, even an "incomplete" esrog may be used.

Missing peel

An esrog has several layers of peel:

(1) An external, very thin, membrane that gives the sheen to the esrog.

(2) The second layer, a green or yellow rind.

(3) A thick, fleshy internal peel.

If the external membrane (1) peels off, leaving the green or yellow rind intact, the esrog is still considered complete and

---

7. There are two basic types of disqualification that apply to an esrog. The first is a disqualification because of *hadar.* The Torah (*Vayikra* 23:40) refers to the esrog as "the fruit of the *hadar* [lit. beautiful] tree." When an esrog lacks this quality (as halachically defined by the *poskim*) it cannot be considered "the fruit of the *hadar* tree" and is thus fundamentally disqualified. Included in this disqualification are the various color changes that disqualify an esrog. This disqualification is generally applied to all the days of Succos.

The second is a disqualification because the esrog is *chaseir,* incomplete. The above-cited verse begins with the Hebrew word וּלְקַחְתֶּם *[ulekachtem],* (And you shall take). The Sages derive from this word that the taking must be a לְקִיחָה תַּמָּה *[lekichah tamah],* a "complete taking." However, since the verse refers only to "taking" on the first day, the disqualification is applied only to the first day and *Yom Tov Sheni.*

8. See page 18.

9. The size of an *issar* is not definitively known. However, it has been conjectured to be between .9 and 1.53 inches (2.3-3.9 cm.).

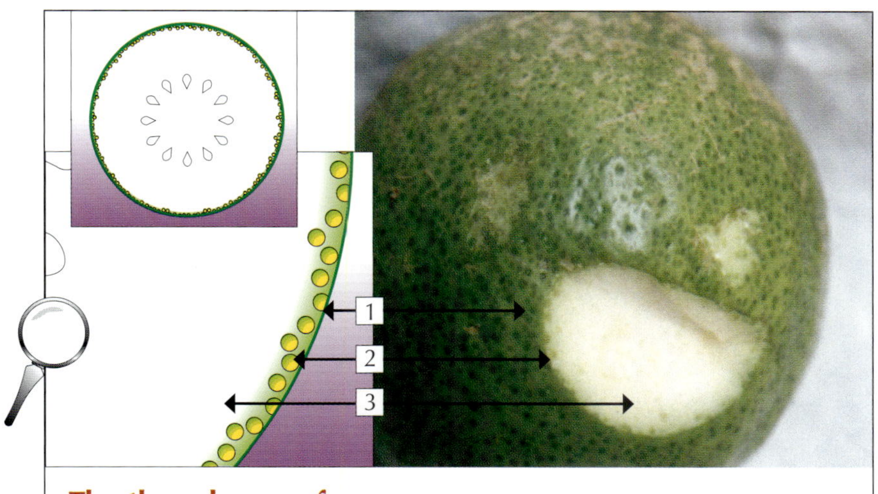

The three layers of an esrog

1. The outer layer is a thin, glossy membrane.
2. The middle layer is green or yellow with eye-like circles.
3. The innermost layer is the thick, white and fleshy peel.

may be used (*Shulchan Aruch* 648:6). In practice, however, it is difficult to be certain that the other parts of the peel are fully intact. Accordingly, a rabbi should always be consulted if any of the external membrane is missing.[10]

If any part of the second layer (2) is missing, *Mishnah Berurah* (§25) considers the esrog incomplete, and disqualifies its use on the first day of Succos (and one using such an esrog on *Yom Tov Sheni* may not recite the *berachah*). According to *Chazon Ish,* however, it may be used unless part of the third layer (3) is missing.

---

10. A number of factors may lead the rabbi to rule leniently in this situation: *Mishnah Berurah* §11 rules that where there is doubt whether flesh is missing, we rule leniently. In addition, several early authorities are of the opinion that an esrog is not considered "incomplete" unless part of the *third* layer is missing (*Rosh,* cited by *Shaar HaTziyun* §27). Although *Shaar HaTziyun* (ibid.) understands *Ran* as disqualifying an esrog when some of the *second* layer is missing, *Chazon Ish* (147:1) asserts that even *Ran* agrees with *Rosh* and that no early authority disqualifies an esrog when only some of the second layer is missing.

When there is doubt [i.e., even an expert cannot determine[11]] whether any part of the second layer (2) is indeed missing, the esrog may be used (*Mishnah Berurah* §11, based on the lenient opinion regarding *chaseir* cited above).

Holes and slits

When a thorn or burr take a bit out of an esrog while the esrog is still on the tree, the esrog is kosher as long as the hole is *completely* covered by scar tissue (*Mishnah Berurah* §10); otherwise it is considered incomplete.

The shape of the mark on the esrog can help determine whether a piece of the esrog is missing.

A long line is the result of a scratch, which generally scrapes off a piece of the esrog. This is when the above rule applies. A deep hole, on the other hand, generally results from a thorn puncturing the esrog, pushing the flesh in without removing

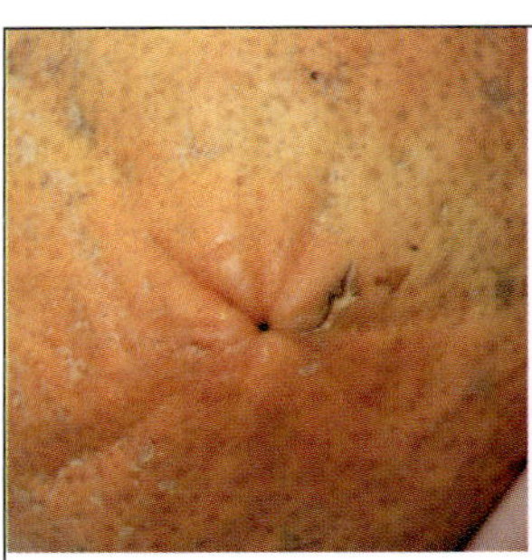

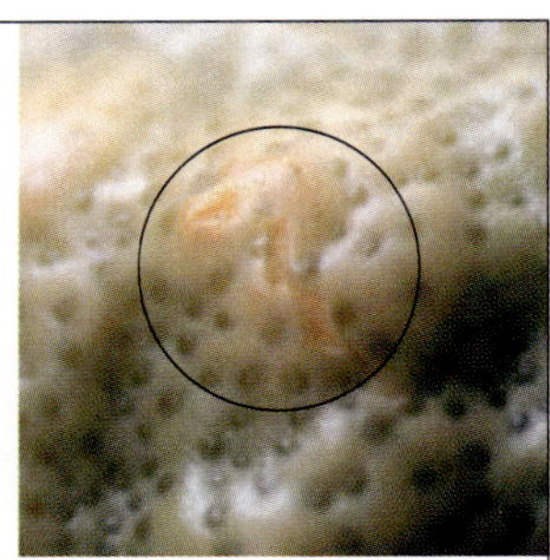

A slit caused by a thorn

Left picture: During the esrog's growth, it was scratched by a thorn. As a result of the scratch, part of the middle layer of the esrog is missing. The resultant scar clearly shows depth and well-defined edges.

Right picture: The indentation has depth, but the sides are smooth. This indicates that the esrog is *not* incomplete.

11. See *Shulchan Aruch, Yoreh De'ah* 98:3.

any of the esrog. An esrog with such a hole is thus fully acceptable, even if the hole is not covered by scar tissue.

Even a long slit, however, does not necessarily indicate that part of the esrog is missing, and the damage may be only on the outer layer, which does not make an esrog "incomplete" in any way. If the slit does not have *both* (a) depth (i.e., it reaches the second layer of the esrog), and (b) well-defined edges, the esrog is considered שָׁלֵם [*shaleim*], complete. In certain cases in which the indentation has depth but not well-defined edges, the sheen of the external membrane can actually be seen in the indentation. This provides additional verification that the esrog is complete.

An indentation caused by an insect

When an insect attaches itself to an esrog at an early stage of growth, it interferes with the esrog's development and causes an indentation. The esrog is not incomplete, and is fully acceptable. (In this picture, the insect already fell off.)

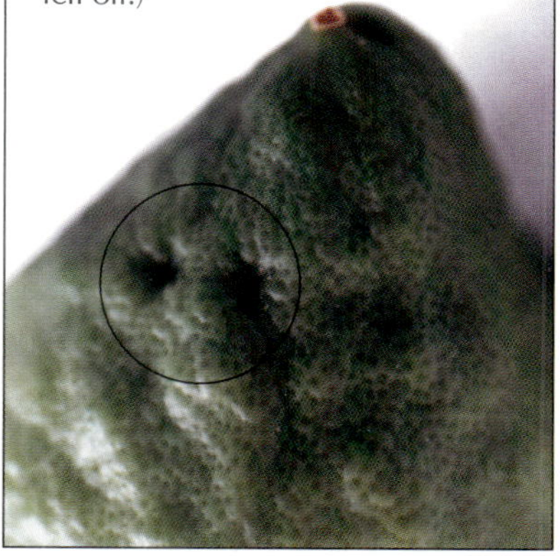

A peeled part which caused a color change was discussed above, page 37.

◆§ The פִּיטָם / *Pitam* and the עֹקֶץ / Stem

A broken *pitam*

The *pitam* is the stemlike growth on the top of an esrog, opposite the actual stem of the esrog, which connects the fruit to the tree. A broken-off *pitam* disqualifies an esrog. The authorities dispute whether the disqualification is one of *hadar* — in which case it is disqualified all seven days of Succos — or of *chaseir* — in which case it is disqualified on the first day, may be used only without a *berachah* on *Yom Tov Sheni,* and may be used on Chol HaMoed even with a *berachah* (*Mishnah Berurah* 649:36; see note 7 on page 42).

If only a portion of the *pitam* is broken, so that part of it remains above the esrog level, the esrog is kosher. However, *Mishnah Berurah* recommends that one should acquire a replacement esrog, in deference to those who maintain that even this is a deficiency in *hadar.*

According to *Kaf HaChaim* (§46) there are two types of *pitam:*

The first — A woody, stem-like protuberance; this is the *pitam* discussed by the *poskim.*

The second — "Found among us in the Land of Israel, there is, at the top of the esrog, a small tip growing out of the esrog itself, to which is attached a dry flowerlike piece"; i.e., the *pitam* is a continuation of the actual esrog. Accordingly, if even part of the *pitam* breaks off, the esrog is incomplete, and it may not

A *pitam* growing out of the esrog itself

In the esrog on the right, the *pitam* is a part of the body of the esrog. Accordingly, if it breaks, the esrog is considered incomplete (*Kaf HaChaim*).

Left is a photograph of that esrog when split. It can be seen that the split *pitam* is a continuation of the esrog.

be used on the first day of Succos. On *Yom Tov Sheni,* it may be used only if another esrog is not reasonably available, and one may not recite the *berachah.*

An esrog that grows without a *pitam*

The *pitam* is the remnant of the fertilized blossom of the esrog tree. Since all esrogim grow from fertilized blossoms, they all have a *pitam* at some point in their development. During the normal course of the development of many esrogim, the pitam dries up and falls off. Since this is part of the regular development of these esrogim, they are considered complete (*Rema* §7[12] and *Mishnah Berurah* §32).

An esrog whose *pitam* fell off during its development can be distinguished from an esrog whose *pitam* falls off later on by a natural indentation, fully covered by scar tissue, that forms in the place of the *pitam.* If such an indentation is present, the esrog is fully acceptable (*Mishnah Berurah* ibid.). [Others are more stringent and allow using the esrog only when the *pitam* fell off at a very early stage. By examining the indentation, an expert can determine the stage at which the *pitam* fell off.]

An indentation in place of the *pitam*

When there is an indentation in the place of the *pitam,* and it is completely covered with scar tissue, the esrog is fully acceptable.

A missing stem

If the stem (*oketz*) of the esrog is missing, leaving only a hole where the stem had been, the esrog is considered

12. Although *Rema* refers to an esrog that "never" had a *pitam,* that is a botanical impossibility, as explained above. Clearly, he means an esrog that loses its *pitam* in the course of its natural development (R' S. Z. Auerbach, cited in *Kashrus Arbaas HaMinim,* p. 27; *Shevet HaLevi* I:177).

incomplete.[13] However, if enough stem remains to cover the entire hole and to fill it so that it is level with the esrog surface, it is still considered to be complete (*Mishnah Berurah* §34). As noted above, an incomplete esrog may be used on all but the first day of Succos [and one using such an esrog on *Yom Tov Sheni* may not recite the *berachah*] (*Rema* 649:5).

The stem

A missing stem

If the stem is missing, the esrog may be used on Chol HaMoed

13. The source for this law is *Succah* 35b. Rabbeinu Chananel there explains that this disqualifies the esrog "because we fear that a piece of the esrog came out with it." This implies that if the stem falls off in circumstances in which no piece of the esrog could have fallen off, the esrog is kosher. Thus, when the esrog is stored with apples to force it to turn yellow and as a result the stem falls off, the esrog would not be disqualified.

Nevertheless, it is not fully clear that Rabbeinu Chananel himself would agree with this leniency. Furthermore, *Rif* (ad loc.) explains the disqualification: "It appears like a hole in which some esrog is missing and thus it is disqualified." This explanation certainly leaves no room for permitting a stem that falls out because of storing with apples. One should not be lenient on this point, in accordance with the simple meaning of the *Shulchan Aruch* and the authorities. Certainly, if there would be room for leniency one of the authorities would have mentioned this fairly common occurrence (R' Refael Reichman *shlita*, in a correspondence with the author).

The Size of an Esrog

The minimum size of a kosher esrog is a כְּבֵיצָה [*kebeitzah*], the size of an average egg (the approximate volume of which is 2.2 fluid ounces) (*Shulchan Aruch* 648:22), but it is appropriate to use an esrog whose volume is no less than 3 fluid ounces (see *Beur Halachah,* citing *Bikkurei Yaakov,* based on the opinion of *Tzelach)*. Nowadays, when esrogim of the larger size are generally easy to obtain, one should follow the latter opinion.

Minimum size of an esrog

The minimum size of an esrog is *kebeitzah,* the size of an egg. According to the preferred opinion, that volume is 3 fluid ounces, which is the approximate volume of the lemon pictured on the left. The relatively small esrog pictured above is considerably larger than 3 fluid ounces.

A Green Esrog

An esrog that is grass-green (dark green) is disqualified (*Shulchan Aruch* §21) because that indicates that the fruit has not yet finished its development (*Mishnah Berurah* §64). If it is lighter than that shade of green it is kosher, because the development is assumed to be complete (ibid.) The nature of our esrogim is to lighten in color as time goes by, even though they have been cut from the tree. This indicates that their development was complete even when they were still dark green. Accordingly, a dark green esrog of this type may be used as well (*Shulchan Aruch* and *Mishnah Berurah* ibid.).[14]

14. *Mishnah Berurah* writes: "The later authorities agree that one should not rely on this leniency, and thus, one should not buy esrogim that have not begun to lighten, lest the esrog remain that shade of green."

Many are nevertheless lenient and use dark green esrogim as well, since *all* our esrogim lighten with time. See also *Teshuvos Chut HaMeshulash* §23 and *Chazon Ish* 148:3.

A Practical Guide to Examining an Esrog

Most disqualifications of an esrog involve the *chotem* (see page 34), since even small spots on the *chotem* can disqualify the esrog. Therefore, begin examining the esrog at the *chotem.* Check whether there are clearly visible black spots or color changes as a result of peeling, since these may disqualify the esrog (provided that they are clearly visible without intense scrutiny). If there are only leaf marks (*bletlach*) there, the esrog is kosher (as long as the leaf marks are not white or another unacceptable color), but they diminish the quality of the esrog.

Next, look at the whole esrog and see if there are any color changes, black spots, missing parts of the peel, slits, or scratches. The details concerning when these disqualify the esrog were explained above. Even when the esrog is not disqualified, you must consider how much they diminish the quality of the esrog.

Other factors that determine the quality of an esrog are:

(a) its size;

(b) its shape;

(c) its color.

Many classic works of Jewish thought mention that one should pray on Tu B'Shvat to merit having a beautiful esrog for the coming Succos.

Lulav

ולקחתם לכם
ביום הראשון
פרי עץ הדר
כפות תמרים
ענף עץ עבות
וערבי נחל

הַתְּיוֹמֶת / The *teyomes*

The *teyomes* is the centermost leaf emerging from the spine (שִׁדְרָה, *shidrah*) of the lulav.

Lulav

◆§ The Fundamental Dispute between *Shulchan Aruch* and *Rema*

There is a fundamental dispute between the *Shulchan Aruch* and the *Rema* which applies to many of the disqualifications that will be discussed in this chapter. According to the *Shulchan Aruch* (645:3; this is also the opinion of the majority of the earlier authorities [*Rishonim*]), the lulav is disqualified only when the majority of its leaves are affected by a disqualifying problem. According to this view, virtually all lulavim (pl. of lulav) available today may be used.[1]

Rema, however, follows the opinion of those *Rishonim* who disqualify the lulav even when only the תְּיוֹמֶת *[teyomes]*, the centermost double leaf — which is the highest of the three central leaves growing out of the top of the central spine (שִׁדְרָה, *shidrah*) of the lulav — is affected.

1. A possible exception to this is the disqualification of a נִקְטַם ראשו, [*niktam rosho*], "a cut-off top" (see below page 71), which may be unacceptable even according to the *Shulchan Aruch*. See *Beur Halachah* to 645:6 s.v. *rov*, who cites a dispute among the authorities concerning this point. As to the הִמְנָק, "*himnak*" split (see below page 59) and see *Beur Halachah* to 645:7 s.v. *nisdak*.

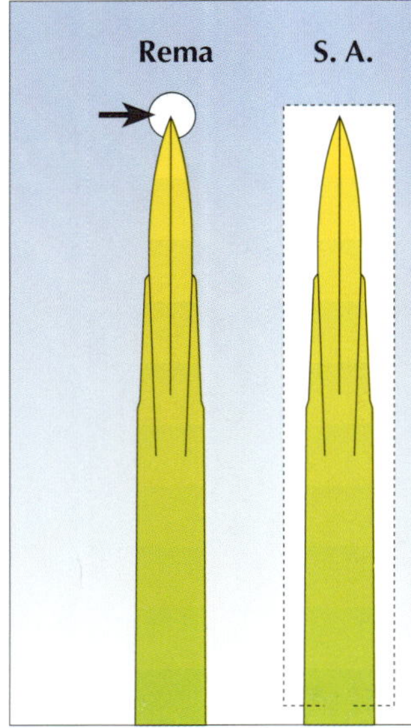

The dispute between *Shulchan Aruch* and *Rema*

According to *Shulchan Aruch (S.A.),* a lulav is not disqualified unless most of the leaves are disqualified (as indicated in the diagram on the right), whereas according to *Rema,* the lulav is disqualified if only the centermost leaf *(תְּיוֹמֶת, teyomes)* is disqualified (as indicated in the diagram on the left).

The accepted Ashkenazi practice accords with the ruling of *Rema*. We will therefore explain all the disqualifications as applying to the *teyomes*.

הַתְּיוֹמֶת / The *teyomes*

Each leaf of a lulav grows as a folded double-leaf, connected in back and unattached in front. These leaves grow out of the sides and top of a spinelike center known as the שִׁדְרָה, *shidrah*. The central double-leaf that grows out of the top of the *shidrah* (usually the middle-most of three central leaves) is known as the *teyomes* (*Rema* 645:3; see picture on page 54).

A split *teyomes*

If the *teyomes* is split most of the way down the leaf (נֶחְלְקָה הַתְּיוֹמֶת, *nechlekah hateyomes)*, the lulav is disqualified for use on the first day of Succos and one using such a lulav on *Yom Tov Sheni*[2] may not recite the *berachah* (*Gra* and *Mishnah*

2. See page 18.

A split *teyomes*
See details in picture on following page.

Berurah). The lulav may be used, with a *berachah,* on Chol HaMoed (*Mishnah Berurah* §17).[3]

When the *shidrah* ends in two leaves rather than three, both are considered the *teyomes*, and even if only one of them is split most of the way, the lulav is disqualified (*Mishnah Berurah* §15).

3. As explained in note 7 in the previous chapter, disqualifications based on *hadar* (beauty) apply to all the days of Succos, whereas disqualifications based on "completeness" apply only on the first day (and when using such species on *Yom Tov Sheni* one does not recite the *berachah).*

Mishnah Berurah rules in accordance with *Magen Avraham* citing *Rabbeinu Yerucham* that a split *teyomes* invalidates the lulav because the lulav is no

The ideal *teyomes*

Some disqualify a *teyomes* with a slight split, reasoning that as the lulav is waved, the split will increase until most (or all) of the *teyomes* is split. Ideally, one should take this view into account (*Rema*; however *Mishnah Berurah* §19 writes that according to the letter of the law it is unnecessary to take this view into account). Although the *Taz* understands that, even according to the stringent opinion, only a split that is a טֶפַח, [*tefach*[4]], handsbreadth, or more in length affects the lulav, the *Chayei Adam* understands this opinion to restrict using a lulav with a split of *any* size in its *teyomes*. Accordingly, many look for a lulav whose *teyomes* is completely closed.

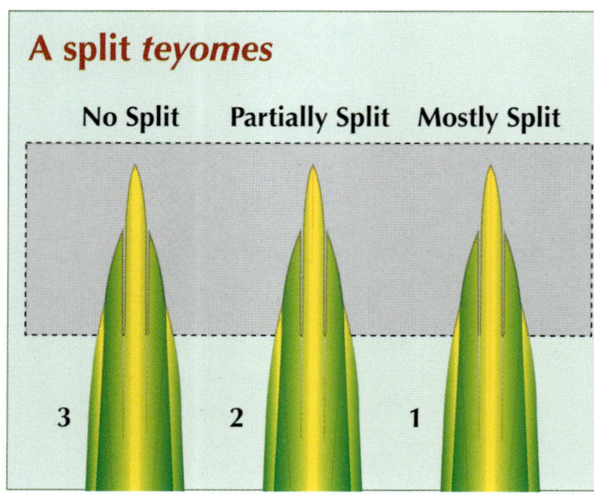

1. When a majority of the *teyomes* is split, the lulav is disqualified for use on the first day of Succos. It may be used on the other days, but is not desirable.
2. When a minority of the *teyomes* is split, the lulav is kosher for use on all the days. Nevertheless, it is not ideal.
3. An ideal lulav has a *teyomes* that is not split at all.

---

longer considered "complete." Accordingly, the disqualification applies only to the first day, and one using such a lulav on *Yom Tov Sheni* would not recite the *berachah*. However, R' Akiva Eiger (*Derush V'Chiddush*, end of Volume 1) cites *Tosafos* (*Succah* 29b s.v. *hikshah*) who imply that this disqualification is one of *hadar*, and disqualifies the lulav for all the days of Succos.

Though one may certainly rely on the lenient opinion (see *Maharsham* cited in *Chaim U'Vrachah* §183), it is appropriate to adopt the stringent approach and treat a split *teyomes* as a disqualification based on *hadar* that disqualifies the lulav for all seven days.

4. A *tefach* is close to 4 inches (about 10 cm.) according to the *Chazon Ish;* about 3.55 inches (9 cm.) according to R' Moshe Feinstein; and 3.15 inches (8 cm.) according to R' Chaim Naeh.

Gluing a split *teyomes*

Several of the later *poskim* (*Maharsham* in *Daas Torah,* R' S. Z. Auerbach, and R' Y. Y. Fisher [in his approbation to *Arbaas HaMinim*]) state that the reason for avoiding a lulav whose *teyomes* is partially split is the fear that the split will spread as the lulav is used. They therefore assert that if a partially-split *teyomes* is glued together, the lulav is perfectly acceptable.[5]

The law regarding a cracked shofar seems to support this opinion. *Shulchan Aruch* (586:8) cites an opinion that disqualifies a shofar with a lengthwise crack of any size, because the force of blowing into the shofar will tend to lengthen the crack. However, if the crack is tightly bound so that it will not lengthen, the shofar is kosher. Apparently, the same can be said regarding a split *teyomes.* According to R' Auerbach (in a conversation with R' Rubin, as related by the latter to the author), this applies only to an ordinary split, not to the הִמְנָק *[himnak]* split discussed in the next paragraph.

GLUE

Many *poskim* advise gluing a partially split *teyomes,* thereby eliminating the problem of a partial split.

◆§ נִסְדַק כְּהִמְנָק / A *Himnak* Split

We have established in the previous section that a partially split *teyomes* is kosher, and the lulav is disqualified only when a majority of the *teyomes* is split. This applies only if the two sides of the *teyomes* remain close to one another. If, however,

5. Others explain that a partial split is avoided not based on a fear that the split might increase, but because of an intrinsic disqualification. According to them, gluing the leaves would not help (see *Hilchos Chag BeChag, Hil. Lulav,* note 15).

the two sides of the *teyomes* are separated, so that they look like two separate leaves, the lulav is disqualified (*Shulchan Aruch* 645:7). This separation is called *nisdak k'himnak,* "split like a *himnak,*" and one should be very careful to avoid it (*Mishnah Berurah* §32).

As long as the two sides of the *teyomes* are close together and continue to look like a single leaf, even if the split is clearly evident, it is not considered a *himnak* split (see *Maharsham*). In certain circumstances (quite uncommon today) the weight of the leaves causes the two parts of the *teyomes* to seem quite far apart. In such a case, if the two parts come together and no longer look like a *himnak* split when the lulav is laid on its side, the lulav is kosher (ibid.)

According to *Magen Avraham* (§6), the disqualification of *himnak* is based on a lack of "completeness" (see note 3 above), so it applies to the first day only, and does not disqualify the lulav on the other days (although one using such a lulav on *Yom Tov Sheni* does not recite the *berachah*). Most authorities rule accordingly (although *Mishnah Berurah* does not cite this ruling of *Magen Avraham*).[6]

Size of a *himnak* split that disqualifies

A *himnak* split of any length disqualifies the lulav.

There is some disagreement, however, regarding how separated the two leaves may be.

Meiri describes the tips of a *himnak* split as "... point[ing] in opposite directions like a compass whose ends are split into two directions." Other *Rishonim*, including *Rif, Rambam, Re'ah, Aruch, Rosh,* and *Tur,* seem to agree.

There are later authorities, however, who ruled more

6. Others base the disqualification on *hadar* (beauty) and therefore disallow using a lulav with such a split on any of the days of Succos (see *Rema* 649:5 and note 3 above; the leniencies cited there — and the conclusion that it is appropriate to adopt the stringent approach — apply here as well).

A *himnak* split

If the two parts of the *teyomes* leaf are split and separated (in the shape of a Y or a V), so that they appear like two separate leaves, the lulav is disqualified on the first day but acceptable on the other days of Succos (but one using such a lulav on *Yom Tov Sheni* does not recite the *berachah*).

stringently in this matter. For instance, *Pri Megadim* (§9) writes, "Separated like a *himnak* disqualifies, even if it is a small amount [in length], and much scrutiny is necessary because it is very common, and care must therefore be taken." *Levushei Serad* writes, "Generally, when the top is split, even if it separates only a little, it is considered a *himnak.*" *Chayei Adam* states, "If the split is wide enough to be visible, that is what the Gemara considers a '*himnak* split.'"

Maharsham disagrees with the *Levushei Serad,* and writes that it is apparent from all the *Rishonim* that to be considered "split like a *himnak*" the two parts must be significantly distant from each other.

An alternate form of *himnak* split

Shaar HaTziyun (§33) cites *Magen Avraham* who writes that even when the *teyomes* is not split at all, but the (doubled) leaves on each side are separated so that they appear to be separate leaves, that too is considered a *himnak* split. *Shaar HaTziyun* (ibid.) writes that according to this opinion, a person examining the integrity of the *teyomes* must make sure to hold the lulav in a way that will not split the adjacent leaves. Nevertheless, the implication of the later *poskim* is that they disagree with *Magen Avraham*. See also *Arbaas HaMinim* (p. 166) who asserts that the implication of the other authorities is that even *Magen Avraham* himself only disqualifies such a lulav if the adjacent leaves are split completely down to the *shidrah*.

☙ קוֹרָא / The *Kora*

A lulav sometimes has a brownish-red covering, generally called *kora* or *moich,* attached over its upper leaves. Although such a lulav is kosher (see *Bikkurei Yaakov* 645:1) and some even consider it preferable, others avoid using such a lulav and look for a lulav with no covering whatsoever.[7]

Kora
A lulav covered with *kora* is kosher. Some authorities prefer such a lulav, others recommend not using it.

In any case, Ashkenazi Jews should remove any *kora* which covers the leaves along the top 3-4 inches of the side of the *shidrah* (ibid.). The reason is that *Rema* (651:9), whose opinions are generally adopted by Ashkenzi

7. R' Y. S. Eliashiv *shlita* is cited as ruling that the covering should be removed. His reasoning is that since a significant minority of lulavim have a split *teyomes* or a *himnak* split, one is required to check for these disqualifications where possible.

Other leading contemporary authorities (including R' Shmuel Wosner and R' N. Karelitz *shlita*) disagree and permit one to leave the *kora* on the lulav. R'

Jews, requires the leaves of a lulav to shake when a person does נַעֲנוּעִים *[naanuim]*, the waving of the lulav. Unless the *kora* is removed from the side leaves, the leaves will not shake when the lulav is waved. (The *Shulchan Aruch* (ibid.), whose opinion is generally followed by those of Sephardi descent, rules that moving the lulav to and fro is sufficient.)

◆§ יָבֵשׁ / A Withered Lulav

A withered lulav is disqualified, but only if most of the lulav's leaves are dry (*Shulchan Aruch* 645:5). "Withered" is defined as the point at which the leaves turn white, with no sign of greenness (ibid.). This degree of dryness is generally found only in a lulav saved from one year to the next. There is a dispute whether the *Raavad* disqualifies a lulav on which just the *teyomes* is dry. Some (*Mishnah Berurah* §22) say that the *Raavad* disqualifies the lulav (even if only a minimal area

---

Y. M. Rubin *shlita* suggests that their reasoning may be that, most of the time, our disqualifying a lulav because of a split *teyomes* or a *himnak* split is based on stringencies adopted due to our uncertainty regarding the exact parameters of the disqualification. Accordingly, one need be stringent only when he actually sees a split of some sort.

Others suggest that the *kora* itself might be considered a proper closing of the split with regard to a split *teyomes*, thereby reducing the need for stringency (see *Bikkurei Yaakov* 645:9; also see *Maamar Mordechai* ad loc., whose view on this matter is not clear).

R' M. Heller *zt"l* said (in a personal communication) that the great halachic authorities of Yerushalayim (including R' Y. C. Sonnenfeld and R' Shmuel Salant *zt"l*) used to use a lulav covered with *kora* even when another fully closed lulav, not covered with *kora*, was available.

See also *Orchos Rabbeinu* II, p. 232, who writes that he heard from R' Chaim Kanievsky that in earlier years the *Chazon Ish* did not remove the *kora* from the lulav and actually sought out a lulav covered with *kora*, since that way he could be certain that the leaves would remain closed. In later years, however, when he heard that the Brisker Rav was stringent and required removing the *kora*, he too would do so.

A tip of the *teyomes* burned by the sun

When the tip of the *teyomes* is burned red by the sun, but the tip remains firm, it is not disqualified.

of the *teyomes* is dry — *Beur Halachah* §7 citing *Ritva*); others maintain that he allows its use.[8]

Chazon Ish (end of §145) writes that it is fairly common to find a lulav burned at its tip by the sun, so that the tip is red-colored. Unlike a withered lulav, however, the leaf is still firm, and this is not included in the category of "*yaveish*."

8. *Raavad* does not explicitly discuss a withered *teyomes*. Rather, he rules that if all the leaves except the *teyomes* are withered, the lulav is kosher.

Mishnah Berurah infers from this that when the middle leaf *is* withered — even if it is only that leaf — the lulav is disqualified. *Bikkurei Yaakov* also understands this to be *Raavad's* opinion, and notes that we find no other *Rishonim* who disqualify such a lulav.

Chazon Ish (end of §145) writes that there is no implication that when only the central leaf *is* withered the lulav is disqualified. *Or Same'ach* (*al hashas*) also disputes this inference, and cites another ruling of the *Raavad* to bolster this assertion.

◆§ קָווּץ / Kavutz

The Talmud (*Succah* 32a) prohibits a lulav that is *kavutz*. *Rashi*, based on the spelling in his version of this passage — קָווּץ — understands this to refer to a lulav with spikelike growths on the *shidrah*. *Ritva*, however, based on the spelling in his version — קָבוּץ — understands it to mean "wrinkled."

Many lulavim (especially those from El-Arish) have leaves (including the central *teyomes* leaf) that end in a zigzag shape on top (see picture below). Although this zigzag shape seems to fit the description of "wrinkled," it is generally considered to be kosher.[9]

It bears noting that lulavim with zigzagging tips often have a split *teyomes* or a *himnak* split, and they must be examined carefully.

Zigzag tip
A lulav whose leaves end in a zigzag shape is kosher, but they should be checked carefully for a split *teyomes* and a *himnak* split.

9. *Kehillos Yaakov* used to say that such lulavim are not merely kosher, but even fulfill ideal requirements (*Orchos Rabbeinu* II, p. 244). The implication of *Shulchan Aruch's* ruling (645:8) concerning *kavutz* is that it is the result of some change in the lulav (e.g., a result of withering) rather than the product of normal growth. Since lulavim that have these zigzag tips grow that way, they are not included in the category of *kavutz*.

◆§ A Single-leafed *Teyomes* and a Partially Single-leafed *Teyomes*

We have already explained that in a lulav each leaf grows as a folded double-leaf (see p. 56). If the *teyomes* grows as a single leaf the lulav is disqualified (*Kol Bo*, cited in *Rema* §3).

Many lulavim grow so that the central leaf is not double-leafed over its entire length, rather one part of the double leaf ends below the top of the other half. Provided that the lower half covers the majority of the higher half, the lulav is not disqualified (see *Graz* 645:9-10).

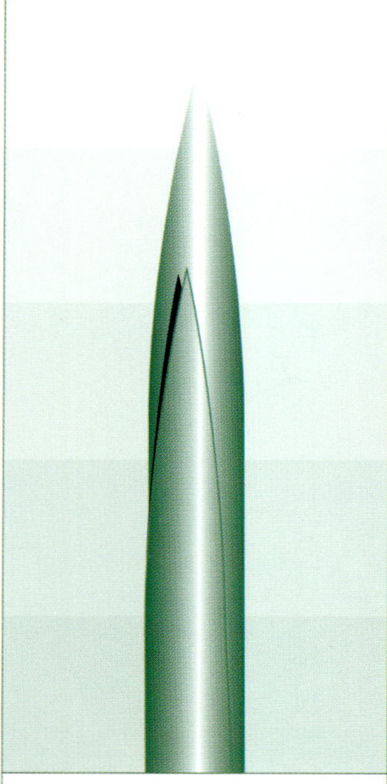

An uneven *teyomes* double-leaf

When one side of the double-leafed ***teyomes*** is shorter than the other, some authorities rule that the lulav is kosher, others disqualify it.

R' N. Karelitz *shlita* rules that stringency in not using such a lulav is in order only when the distance between the two sides is unusual enough to warrant notice. When the distance is only one of millimeters, however, the lulav is fully acceptable (*Maadanei Shlomo* p. 81). A similar ruling was issued by *Kehillos Yaakov* ("the *Steipler*") as cited in *Orchos Rabbeinu* II, p. 235.

R' Y. S. Elyashiv *shlita* (as cited by R' Y. M. Rubin *shlita*), however, maintains that the lulav is acceptable only when one side is minimally shorter than the other.

Sometimes the *teyomes* is fully double-leafed in height, but the two sides of the leaf are not the same width. As long as the narrower leaf covers more than half of the wider

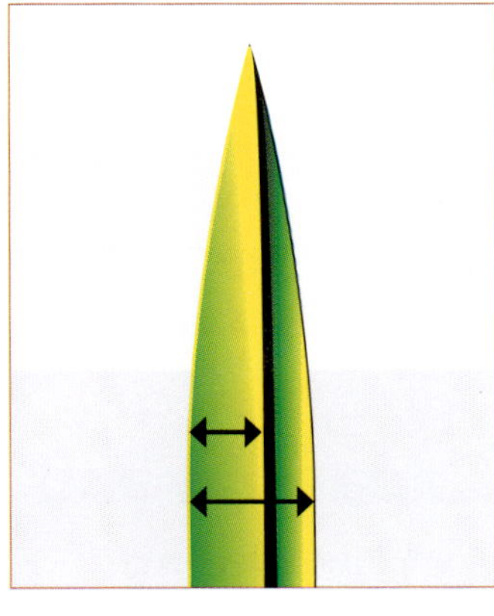

An uneven *teyomes* double leaf

When one side of the double-leafed ***teyomes*** is narrower than the other, the lulav is kosher if the narrower half covers most of the width of the wider half.

leaf, the lulav is not disqualified (*Kehillos Yaakov*, as cited in *Orchos Rabbeinu* II, p. 235; R' S. Z. Auerbach; R' Y. S. Eliashiv, as cited in *Kashrus Arbaas HaMinim*, p. 141).

◈ The Length of a Lulav

The preferred minimum length of a lulav is four טְפָחִים [*tefachim*], handbreadths (*Shulchan Aruch* 650). According to the *Chazon Ish*, this equals 15.75 inches (39 cm.); according to R' Moshe Feinstein this is 14.17 inches (36 cm.); and according to R' Chaim Naeh this equals 12.6 inches (32 cm.)

The length is measured on the *shidrah* (the spinelike core) from the point at the bottom where leaves begin to branch

The length of the lulav

The preferred minimum length of the lulav is four *tefachim* (12.6-14.75 inches). This length is measured from the point where the leaves branch out to the top of the *shidrah*.

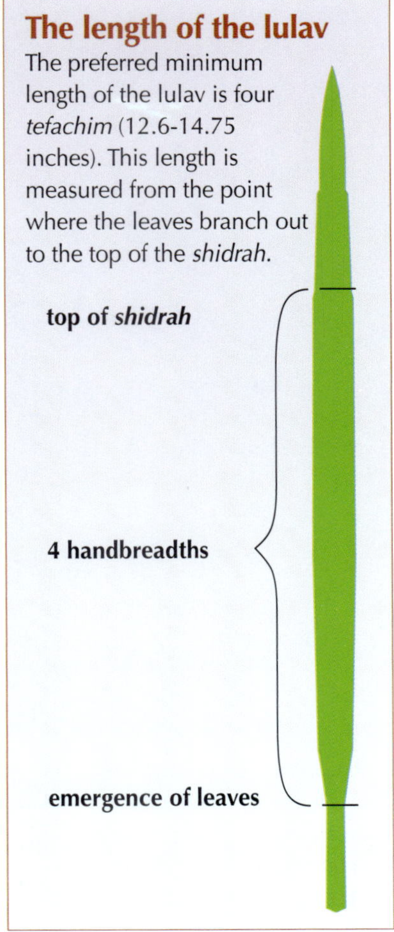

out until the point on top of the *shidrah* where the central leaf emerges. The upper leaves are not included in this measurement, and there is no requisite length for them. By the same token, if leaves at the bottom of the *shidrah* were removed, one must begin measuring from the point that leaves actually begin branching out from the *shidrah*.

◆ Positioning the הֲדַסִּים / Hadassim and עֲרָבוֹת / Aravos Alongside the Lulav

Shulchan Aruch (650:1) states: "The length of the *hadas* and of the *aravah* is three *tefachim* (handbreadths), and the length of the lulav's *shidrah* is four *tefachim* (handbreadths),

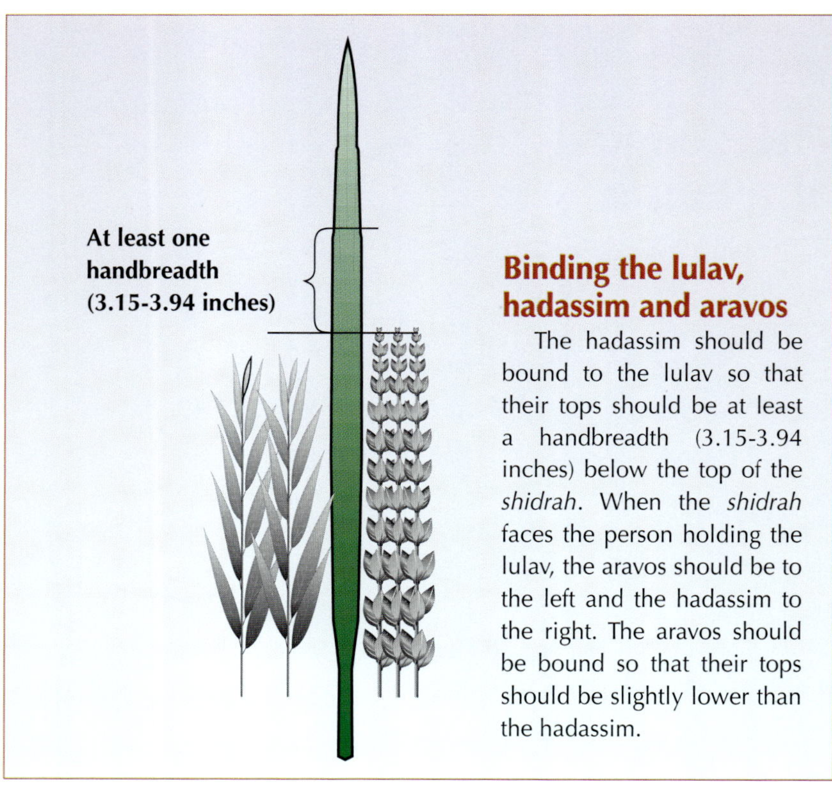

Binding the lulav, hadassim and aravos

The hadassim should be bound to the lulav so that their tops should be at least a handbreadth (3.15-3.94 inches) below the top of the *shidrah*. When the *shidrah* faces the person holding the lulav, the aravos should be to the left and the hadassim to the right. The aravos should be bound so that their tops should be slightly lower than the hadassim.

so that the *shidrah* of the lulav should emerge one *tefach* (handbreadth) above the *hadas*." Thus, in addition to the length requirement for the lulav itself, the *shidrah* of the lulav should extend one *tefach* (handbreadth) [according to the *Chazon Ish*: 3.94 inches (10 cm.); R' Moshe Feinstein: 3.55 inches (9 cm.); R' Chaim Naeh: 3.15 inches (8 cm.)] above the top of the *hadas*. Needless to say, the central leaves emerging from the top of the *shidrah* will extend even higher.

✂ Bent Central Leaf

It is fairly common for the tip of the *teyomes* to curve forward; this is referred to by the Yiddish term *knepl* (button). Such lulavim are kosher (*Shulchan Aruch* 645:9; see *Darchei Moshe* 645). *Rosh* (*She'eilos U'Teshuvos HaRosh* 24:10) writes that he prefers such lulavim "because their leaves are not split and the *teyomes* is complete."

Mishnah Berurah notes that though some *Rishonim*, including *Ritva* and *Ran*, disqualify a lulav with such a *teyomes*,

The central leaf bends down
Some authorities disqualify this, but the accepted custom is to permit its use, in accordance with the ruling of *Shulchan Aruch*.

The central leaf bends forward
Such a lulav is acceptable according to all opinions.

the custom is to permit it in accordance with the ruling of *Shulchan Aruch*. Nevertheless, many people use only lulavim whose top leaves are perfectly straight.[10]

עָקוּם / A Bent Lulav

When the *shidrah* of a lulav is curved back, i.e., toward itself, it is kosher, since it grows that way (*Shulchan Aruch* ibid. :8). If it curves in any other direction it is not kosher, but it is considered *akum,* bent, only if it is — in the words of the *Beis Yosef,* citing *Rashi* and *Rambam* — "curved like a sickle." It is rare to find a lulav with such a great degree of curvature.

◂ A curved lulav
A slightly curved lulav is kosher. However, if it is greatly curved in any direction other than backwards, it is disqualified.

10. There are two kinds of "bent forward": (a) totally bent and facing down; and (b) bent forward but facing straight ahead (see pictures on previous page).

It is only regarding the first type (bent forward and facing down) that some are stringent, although *Shulchan Aruch* permits its use (as is the custom). Regarding the second type, however, it is not considered a "bent-over lulav" and all permit its use (verbal response of R' M. Heller *zt"l*). Accordingly, it would seem that such lulavim are preferable, for they are not disqualified according to *Ran* and *Ritva*, and have the advantage of having unsplit leaves. It should also be noted that when the central leaf bends all the way down to the center of the lulav it is disqualified because it lacks *"hadar."*

נִקְטַם רֹאשׁוֹ / A Lulav With a Cut-off Top

A lulav whose top is cut off is not kosher (*Shulchan Aruch* 645:6). This is true even if only the top of the central leaf is cut off (*Rema* ad loc.). The disqualification is one of *hadar* (*Rashi* to *Mishnah Succah* 29), and thus it applies for all seven days.

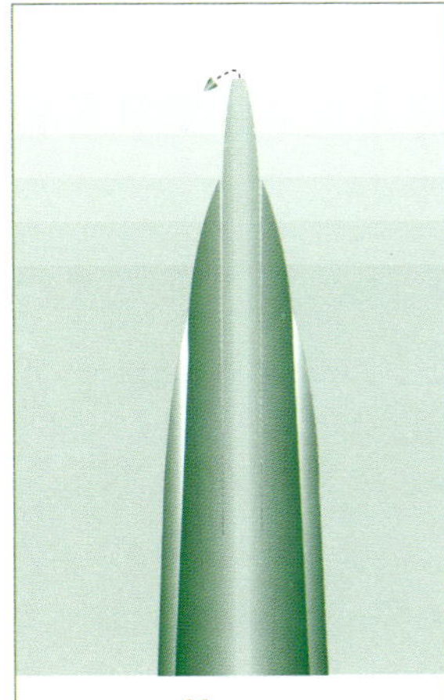

Cut-off top

If any part of the top of the central leaf is cut off, the lulav is disqualified.

How much must be cut off

Even if only a slight amount of the lulav is cut off, the lulav is disqualified (see *Mishnah Berurah* §28). "One should be careful in this matter and examine the lulav well to ascertain that nothing was cut off, and this is easily recognizable" (*Bikkurei Yaakov*).

Nevertheless, as long as the cut is not apparent under close scrutiny, the lulav is not disqualified (R' S. Z. Auerbach in *Maadanei Shlomo,* p. 82; ruling of R' N. Karelitz *shlita*).[11]

When no other lulav is reasonably available, it is permitted to recite the *berachah* on a lulav which had the top of its *teyomes* cut off (*Rema*), but only if a majority of the leaf remains (*Mishnah Berurah* §30).

11. It has been claimed that an uncut central leaf has an elliptical indentation at its top (visible under a magnifying glass) which proves its integrity. Nevertheless, some lulavim whose central leaf was never cut do not have this indentation.

When there is doubt as to whether the central leaf was cut, the lulav is kosher because of a סְפֵק סְפֵיקָא [*sfek sfeka*], double doubt, principle: Perhaps a lulav is only disqualified when the tops of most of its leaves are cut; and even if one cut leaf also disqualifies the lulav, perhaps this is only when most of the top is cut [see *Shulchan Aruch* 645:6, *Mishnah Berurah* §6 and *Shaar HaTziyun* §28] (comment of R' S. Sheinelson *shlita*).

Broken needlelike top

Many lulavim end in a needlelike projection above the top leaf. If only this part is broken off the lulav is kosher *(Ikrei Hadat* 33:21; *Chazon Ish* ruled similarly, see *Hilchos Chag BeChag* 7).

hadassim

ולקחתם לכם
ביום הראשון
פרי עץ הדר
כפות תמרים
ענף עץ עבות
וערבי נחל

hadassim

מְשֻׁלָּשׁ / Triple-leaved

The Torah (*Vayikra* 23:40) states: "You shall take for yourselves ... branches of a cordlike tree (עֲנַף עֵץ עָבֹת, *anaf eitz avos*)." The Talmud (*Succah* 32b) explains that this verse refers to the myrtle (hadas, pl. hadassim), the leaves of which cover the branches (an alternate translation for *eitz*) and are plaited like cords *(avos)* and like ropes, i.e., it has a braidlike form in that its leaves overlap one another (*Rashi* ad loc.)

To be considered "braidlike" (thereby fulfilling the "עָבֹת, *avos*" requirement), the hadas must have three leaves close to each other in one circle, so that one is not lower than the other.

Defining "in one circle" for a triple-leaved hadas

The halachic authorities differ in their definition of "triple-leaved." Some assert that it is only necessary that the three leaves recognizably belong to the same level (see illustration on next page), and this is the custom handed down to the halachic authorities of Yerushalayim (heard from R' M. Heller *zt"l*;[1]

1. R' S. Z. Auerbach used to look at the hadas from a bit of a distance and without scrutiny, and as long as it appeared triple-leaved he would say that that was sufficient (*Maadanei Shlomo,* p. 87).

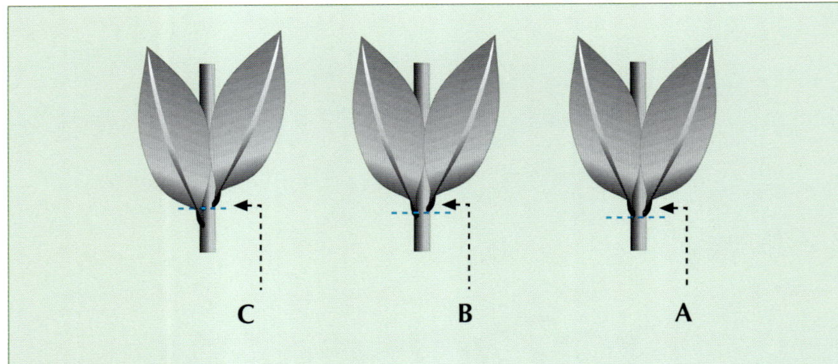

In one circle

A hadas can be considered *"meshulash"* as long as the three leaves seem to be at the same level (as in all the diagrams above). Others require that the stem of all three leaves actually connect to the branch at the same level, which means that a level line would connect some point of the stems of all three leaves. According to them, **B** is acceptable but **C** is not.

R' S. Wosner, cited in *MiBeis HaLevi,* Vol. II, Tishrei 5753). Others, including some of the prominent contemporary authorities, scrutinize the hadas to make certain that each set of three leaves emerges from the same level on the branch.

Even according to this latter view, however, as long as a level line would connect some point of the "stem" of the individuals leaves, that is sufficient, and it is not necessary for the three leaves to emerge from exactly the same height on the branch (*Chazon Ish,* cited in R' Chaim Greineman *shlita*'s *Chiddushim U'Veurim al Maseches Succah,* 5; R' S. Z. Auerbach, in his approbation to *Arbaas HaMinim*).

הֲדַס שׁוֹטֶה / *Hadas shoteh*

When each level has two leaves emerging from one point and a third leaf emerging above or below that point, it is called a *"hadas shoteh."* A *shoteh* is a fool who cannot even walk a straight line; similarly, the leaves do not follow a straight line (*Shulchan Aruch* 646:3). A *hadas shoteh* cannot be used on

Hadas shoteh

The third leaf at each level emerges from a different level. This hadas is disqualified for use on any of the days of Succos.

any of the days of Succos (*Beur Halachah* §1).

The length of hadassim

The minimum length of a hadas branch is 2½ *tefachim,* handbreadths, though some opinions require that it be three handbreadths. The preferred custom is to require three (*Shulchan Aruch* 650), though one can rely on the shorter size when necessary (*Mishnah Berurah* §8). Three handbreadths equals 11.8 inches (30 cm.) according to *Chazon Ish;* 10.63 inches (27 cm.) according to R' Moshe Feinstein; and 9.45 inches (24 cm.) according to R' Chaim Naeh.

The length of the hadas is measured up the height of the branch itself, and the leaves that rise above the branch are not counted (*Mishnah Berurah* §1). Only disqualifications within the required three-handbreadth length disqualify the hadas for use (*Shaar HaTziyun* §3). Ideally, the top three-handbreadths of the hadas should be fully triple-leaved, as discussed above.

A majority (lengthwise)

Although, ideally, a hadas should be triple-leaved across three full handbreadths of its length, as long as most of its length (more than 1½ handbreadths) is triple-leaved, it is kosher, and one using it may recite the *berachah (Shulchan Aruch HaRav* §3). This applies even when this majority is in the middle of the hadas, and not at the top (*Rema* §5).

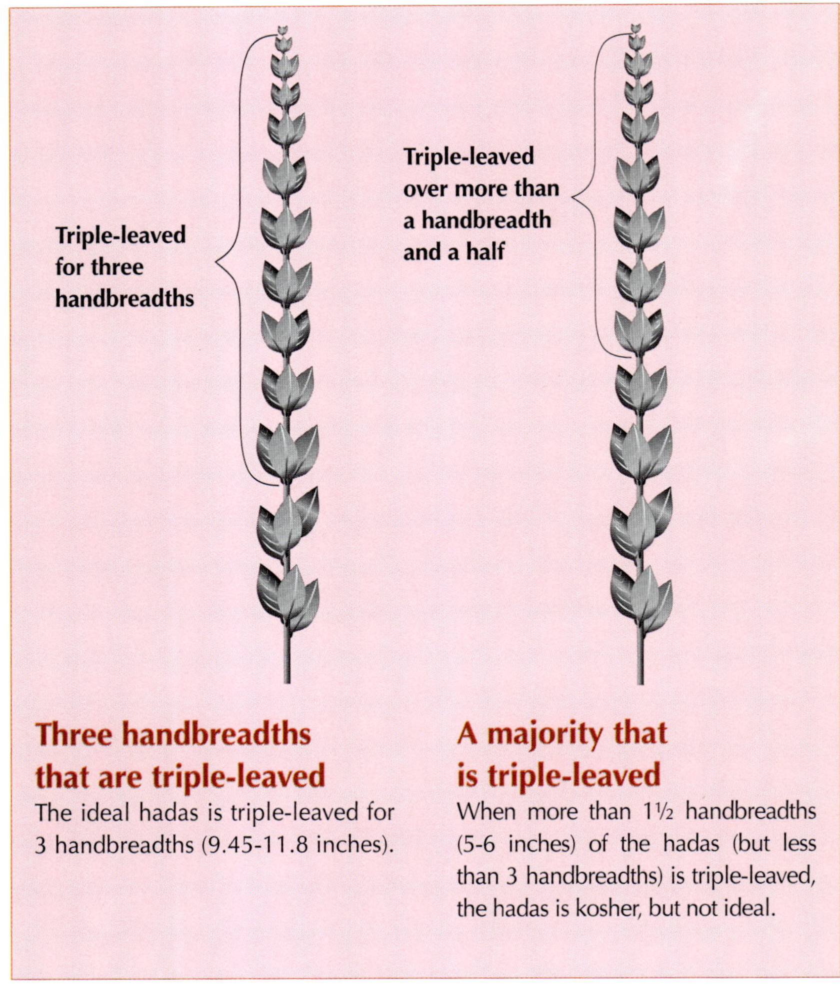

Three handbreadths that are triple-leaved
The ideal hadas is triple-leaved for 3 handbreadths (9.45-11.8 inches).

A majority that is triple-leaved
When more than 1½ handbreadths (5-6 inches) of the hadas (but less than 3 handbreadths) is triple-leaved, the hadas is kosher, but not ideal.

Even if all the leaves fall off part of a hadas, as long as most of the hadas remains triple-leaved it is still acceptable, (see illustration on next page).

Missing rows

If an area along the height of the hadas is not triple-leaved, one measures the triple-leaved portions above and below the missing rows. If at least 1½ handbreadths are triple-leaved, the hadas is acceptable if a replacement is not available.

If the combined three-leaved area covers a full handbreadth, it may be considered similar to a completely triple-leaved hadas in that it is fully kosher, albeit not ideal (heard from R' Y. S. Eliashiv *shlita*).[2] Nevertheless, many specifically seek a hadas that is fully triple-leaved, without any break.

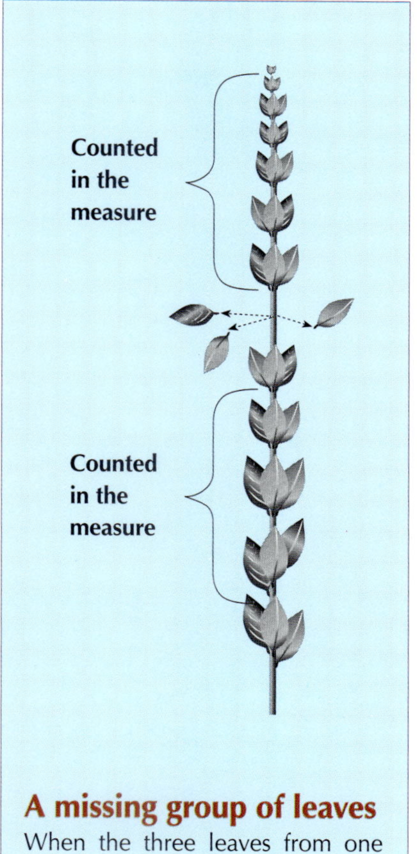

A missing group of leaves
When the three leaves from one level fall out in the middle of the hadas, we measure the triple-leaved portions above and below that level. When the total is more than 1½ handbreadths the hadas is kosher, though not ideal.

Missing leaves down the side

When a hadas that had been fully triple-leaved loses one leaf from each level, so that only two leaves per level remain, its status is the subject of dispute. Some permit its use, based on the principle of רֻבּוֹ כְּכֻלּוֹ, [*rubo kechulo*], a majority [of leaves at each level] is considered complete. Others disqualify it because it lacks

2. This case is different than the one discussed by *Pri Megadim* (cited in *Beur Halachah* §5, end of s.v. *l'ikuva*), because the case discussed by *Pri Megadim* is one in which most of the hadas is not triple-leaved. See, however, *Ran* who cites the *Geonim* who require that the hadas be fully triple-leaved, writing that if even one leaf falls off, the hadas is disqualified. His implication is that it is disqualified even when there is a combined three handbreadths that is triple-leaved.

the cordlike quality of *avos* (see the beginning of this section). In accordance with the view of several later authorities, such hadassim may be used if others are not available (*Mishnah Berurah* §18).

If part of a leaf tears off and most of the leaf remains, it is considered to be a complete leaf.[3]

One leaf missing at several levels

When one of the three leaves is missing at several levels, it is questionable whether the hadas can be considered "triple-leaved." When necessary, one may rely on the lenient opinion that considers it as if it were still triple-leaved.

Partially missing leaf

When part of a leaf is missing, it is considered whole if the majority of the leaf remains.

3. See *Mor U'Ketziah,* cited in *Shaarei Teshuvah* 646:3, who requires that the leaves of the hadas cover the branch in such a way that the leaves of one level overlap the leaves of the level above it. Nevertheless, many authorities dispute this view. See *Bikkurei Yaakov* 11 who writes that it is preferable to follow this view, but the hadas is nevertheless kosher when this is not the case. *Chazon Ish* (146:28) writes that according to the accepted rule that it is sufficient for a majority of the hadas to be *meshulash,* it is similarly acceptable for most of the branch to be covered by leaves; hence the ruling of *Mor U'Ketziah* is difficult.

Other Issues

A withered hadas

A withered hadas is generally kosher. It is only disqualified as יָבֵשׁ [*yaveish*], dry, when: (a) the leaves break when touched by a fingernail, and (b) the leaves lose their green color and begin to turn white (*Shulchan Aruch* 6-7). This stage of dryness is quite rare for hadassim that grew in the current year (*Mishnah Berurah* §31).

Cut-off top

Some permit the use of a hadas whose top was cut off (נִקְטַם, *niktam*); others disqualify it. It is preferable to be stringent in the matter (*Shulchan Aruch* 10). Nevertheless, if only the upper leaves — and not the branch — are cut, it is not considered *niktam* (*Rema* ad loc.).

Cut-off top

When the top of the hadas branch is missing, the hadas should preferably not be used.

Caution when binding the hadas!

Hadassim and aravos are usually bound to the lulav by means of a holder made of woven lulav leaves with one central hole for the lulav and small compartments into which the hadassim and aravos are inserted. When the hadassim are inserted into their compartment, leaves are often torn off. It would be a pity for a person to expend time and effort in finding a fully triple-leaved hadas only to ruin that ideal hadas himself by causing leaves to fall off. To avoid this problem, one should insert the hadassim (as well as the aravos) into their compartment slowly and carefully, pressing down on the edge of the compartment to widen the hole. In this manner the hadassim can be inserted without any leaves falling off. (If the top three handbreadths of the hadas extend from the holder and are triple-leaved, there is no need to be concerned about the lower leaves falling off.)

It should be noted that although there is no obligation to use a holder, it helps to prevent problems caused by handling, and such holders are used by many leading rabbinic authorities.

aravos

ולקחתם לכם
ביום הראשון
פרי עץ הדר
כפות תמרים
ענף עץ עבות
וערבי נחל

Aravos

The Length of Aravos

The preferred length of an aravah is the same as that of hadassim — three *tefachim* (handbreadths) (*Shulchan Aruch* 651). Three *tefachim* equals 11.8 inches (30 cm.) according to *Chazon Ish;* 10.63 inches (27 cm.) according to R' Moshe Feinstein; and 9.45 inches (24 cm.) according to R' Chaim Naeh. This length is measured up the stem, preferably starting from the base of the lowest leaf. The height of leaves that extend above the stem is not included in this measurement.

The length of the aravah
The aravah should be three *tefachim* long (9.45 — 11.8 inches).

נָשְׁרוּ עָלָיו / Missing Leaves

Missing leaves

Ideally, all the leaves of the top three *tefachim* of the aravah should be intact. If only some of the leaves fell off or dried out, the aravah is still kosher. However, if most of the leaves fell off or dried out, the aravah is disqualified.

If most leaves of the three upper handbreadths of the aravah fall off, the aravah is disqualified. If only some of the leaves fall off, the aravah is kosher *(Shulchan Aruch* 647: 2); some say that the aravah is kosher לְכַתְּחִלָּה [*lechatchilah*], without reservation *(Eliyahu Rabbah)*, while others maintain that it is better not to use such an aravah (*Magen Avraham).* Since aravos (plural of aravah) are generally easily available, one should follow the latter opinion *(Mishnah Berurah* §11*).*

As with the hadassim, care should be taken to keep the aravos intact when placing them in their holder (see p. 82).

יָבֵשׁ וְכָמוּשׁ / A Dried Aravah

When most of the leaves of an aravah are dried (יָבֵשׁ, *yaveish*) or withered (כָּמוּשׁ, *kamush*), it is disqualified (*Shulchan Aruch* 647:2; *Mishnah Berurah* §7). A leaf is considered "withered" if there is no green left in it. As long as there is some greenness in the leaf, even if the touch of a fingernail would crack it, the leaf is considered intact (*Shaar HaTziyun* §6). It is nevertheless preferable to use aravos that are not at all withered. This may require that one change aravos every few days.

נִקְטַם רֹאשׁוֹ / A Cut-off Top

An aravah may not be used if the top of its stem is cut off (*Shulchan Aruch* ibid.). The top leaf, however, has the same rule as any other missing leaf (*Mishnah Berurah* §10), and its being cut does not disqualify the aravah.

לַבְלוּב / A small top leaf

Many aravos have a young leaf, colloquially referred to as a *"lavluv,"* growing out of the top of the stem. Though the presence of a *lavluv* guarantees that the top of the aravah was not cut off, an aravah with this leaf is no more preferable than any other aravah with an intact top.

Cut-off top leaf

If the top leaf falls off, the aravah is kosher. If the top of the stem is cut off, however, the aravah is disqualified.

Lavluv

The small young leaf growing out of the top of the stem indicπates that the top of the stem is intact.

General Laws of the Four Species

General Laws of the Four Species

◆§ Binding the Species

There is no formal obligation to bind the lulav, hadassim, and aravos together. Indeed, if one were to have all the Four Species in front of him and would pick up each of them one at a time, he would fulfill the basic mitzvah (*Shulchan Aruch* 651: 12). It is nevertheless a mitzvah to bind together the lulav, the three hadassim, and the two aravos because of the Biblical precept (*Shemos* 15:2): זֶה קֵלִי וְאַנְוֵהוּ, *This is my G-d and I shall adorn him,* i.e., because the halachah considers it to look nicer that way (*Mishnah Berurah* §7).

According to *Shulchan Aruch* (ibid. :1), they should be tied together by means of a permanent (double) knot. Nevertheless, the prevalent practice is to use the holder of woven lulav leaves, known as the *koishekel,* in place of a knot (see *Mishnah Berurah* §8).

It is customary to tie three rings [made of lulav leaves] around the lulav (*Rema* 651:1), but, at the very least, one ring should be tied (*Mishnah Berurah* §14). Some have the custom to tie one of the three rings around the *koishekel* holding the hadassim and aravos; others tie three rings around the lulav itself and tie a fourth ring around the *koishekel.*

The rings should be positioned below the uppermost *tefach* of the *shidrah* of the lulav, so that the leaves of the lulav can be shaken properly (ibid.).

One should hold the lulav so that the *shidrah* of the lulav faces him (*Mishnah Berurah* 650:8). The hadassim should then be placed in the holder to the right of the lulav's *shidrah*, and the aravos to the left,[1] with the tops of the hadassim extending higher than the tops of the aravos (*Rema* 651:1).

☙ Purchasing Four Species for Children

A father is required to train his minor children to do mitzvos. Thus, when a child is old enough to know how to properly shake a lulav, his father is obligated to acquire one for him (*Shulchan Aruch* 657). *Mishnah Berurah* (§4), however, asserts that it is sufficient for a father to give his own Four Species to his son to use after the father himself fulfills his requirement. However, a father who will observe *Yom Tov Sheni* must take care not to assign ownership of his Four Species to his minor child on the first day, since the father needs them to be "his" on *Yom Tov Sheni* as well.

It is preferable for a child to have his own Four Species when he goes to shul to *daven,* so that he can wave the lulav at the appropriate times (ibid.).

1. The same applies to left-handed people (see *Mishnah Berurah* ibid.; see also R' Chaim Kanievsky *shlita's* pamphlet for lefties).

While the Four Species purchased for a child must be kosher (*Beur Halachah* op. cit.), they need not be of the same high quality that an adult would choose for himself.

Many refrain from purchasing a set of Four Species for their minor children because of the expense and difficulty involved in finding a high quality set. Yet, for purposes of *chinuch* (training a minor), even a set that is not מְהֻדָּר *[mehudar]*, beautiful, is sufficient. Generally, these are easily available at a reasonable price, and in purchasing them a father fulfills his obligation to train his son in performing mitzvos.

We are listing several deficiencies that lower the quality of the species without disqualifying them (even for adults). This should make it easier to purchase kosher, easily available, and inexpensive species for a minor:

A lulav whose central double leaf is open less than halfway is kosher (and the split leaves may be glued together to prevent them from splitting further, as explained on page 59).

A hadas need be triple-leaved only across a majority of its length, which is about 5-6 inches (see page 77).

An esrog is kosher even if it has many leaf marks, and even if they are on the upper part of the esrog.

◆§ The First Day of Succos vs. the Rest of the Days

In commanding us to take the Four Species, the Torah tells us: וּלְקַחְתֶּם לָכֶם בַּיּוֹם הָרִאשׁוֹן, *And you shall take for yourselves on the first day* (*Vayikra* 23:40). Thus, our *mitzvah d'Oraisa* (Biblical requirement) to take the Four Species applies only to the first day of Succos. The verse continues, וּשְׂמַחְתֶּם לִפְנֵי ה׳ אֱלֹקֵיכֶם שִׁבְעַת יָמִים, *and you shall rejoice before Hashem, your G-d, seven days*. This is understood as teaching that "before Hashem," i.e., in the *Beis HaMikdash*, the mitzvah applies for seven days.

When the *Beis HaMikdash* was destroyed, the Sages instituted taking the Four Species everywhere for seven days, in commemoration of the *Beis Hamikdash* (*Mishnah, Succah* 41a).

However, when the Sages made this enactment, they stipulated that several of the disqualifications that apply on the first day would not apply on the other days. They include:

שָׁאוּל, Borrowed: It is understood that when the Torah states, *"And you shall take* לָכֶם*, for yourselves,* בַּיּוֹם הָרִאשׁוֹן*, on the first day...,"* it is telling us that on the first day one must use Four Species that *belong to him*. Accordingly, on the first day — and on *Yom Tov Sheni* — one may not use Four Species borrowed from one's friend, unless his friend gives them to him to own. (One can, however, have a friend give him the Four Species on the condition that he will then give them back to his friend to reacquire.) On the other days of Succos, however, there is no disqualification of "borrowed."

חָסֵר, Incomplete: If any of the required parts of one of the species is missing (e.g., a piece of the esrog or the top of the central leaf in a lulav), it is disqualified for use on the first day but acceptable on the other days;[2] on *Yom Tov Sheni* it would be used without reciting the *berachah*. This results from an alternate reading of the above-cited verse, וּלְקַחְתֶּם לָכֶם בַּיּוֹם הָרִאשׁוֹן*, And you shall take for yourselves on the first day ..."* The Hebrew for *"And you shall take"* is *"Ulekachtem,"* which alludes to לְקִיחָה תַּמָּה [*lekichah tamah*], a complete taking, i.e., one that is not deficient. Since this is stated with regard to the "first day," it applies to the first day only. Here too, on *Yom Tov Sheni* one using Four Species that are deficient would use them without reciting the *berachah*.

2. On the other days it lacks the element of "This is my G-d and I shall adorn Him" mentioned above, but it is not one of the requirements for fulfilling the mitzvah (*Raavad; Meiri*).

הָדָר, ***Hadar*:** The *Rishonim* (early authorities) disagree as to whether the disqualifications based on *hadar,* "beauty" (as defined by the halachah) apply to Chol HaMoed as well. The majority view, expressed by *Rambam* and *Shulchan Aruch,* is that these disqualifications do not apply. The other view, expressed by *Rosh* and *Rema* and followed by Ashkenazi Jews, is to require *hadar* for all the days of Succos.

Not the species described in the Torah: A disqualification based on being different from the species described in the Torah (e.g., a grafted esrog, an esrog so green that the fruit is clearly not fully developed, a hadas that is not triple-leaved or missing most of its leaves [and thereby not being *avos,* braided like a cord, see page 75) applies to all the days of Succos.

Yom Tov Sheni — The Second Day

Jews who live outside of Israel keep a second day of Succos similar to the first. This day is known as *Yom Tov Sheni* (the second festival day), which is how it is referenced throughout this work. In general, all disqualifications that apply to the first day apply to the second day as well. It is nevertheless not necessary to be stringent about a minimal deficiency, since some permit a minimal deficiency even on the first day (see *Mishnah Berurah* 648:8).

If another, fully acceptable set of Four Species are not reasonably available, one may take species with first-day disqualifications. He may not, however, recite the *berachah* over them (*Shulchan Aruch* 649:5 and *Mishnah Berurah* §50; see there for the reason).

This volume is part of
THE ARTSCROLL SERIES®
an ongoing project of
translations, commentaries and expositions
on Scripture, Mishnah, Talmud, Halachah,
liturgy, history, the classic Rabbinic writings,
biographies and thought.

For a brochure of current publications
visit your local Hebrew bookseller
or contact the publisher:

Mesorah Publications, ltd
4401 Second Avenue
Brooklyn, New York 11232
(718) 921-9000